Top 10 Reasons
Why You Should Read This Book

10. You want to learn about the path that we took at Zappos to get to over $1 billion in gross merchandise sales in less than ten years.

9. You want to learn about the path I took that eventually led me to Zappos, and the lessons I learned along the way.

8. You want to learn from all the mistakes we made at Zappos over the years so that your business can avoid making some of the same ones.

7. You want to figure out the right balance of profits, passion, and purpose in business and in life.

6. You want to build a long-term, enduring business and brand.

5. You want to create a stronger company culture, which will make your employees and coworkers happier and create more employee engagement, leading to higher productivity.

4. You want to deliver a better customer experience, which will make your customers happier and create more customer loyalty, leading to increased profits.

3. You want to build something special.

2. You want to find inspiration and happiness in work and in life.

1. You ran out of firewood for your fireplace. This book makes an excellent fire starter.

Praise for DELIVERING Happiness

"A zippy, pleasant read ... [I hope] that the micro-managers of the world will read Tony's book and realize that happiness and profit can be best friends."　　　　　　　　　　　—*Fast Company*

"Compelling ... an uplifting tale of entrepreneurial success, personal growth, and redemption."　　　　　　　—*Publishers Weekly*

"This book is awesome. How Tony and Zappos grew to $1 billion in gross revenue in ten years is just the beginning. From fundraising to finding happiness, from actual e-mails to checklists, it covers it all. Intensely personal and intensely practical."
　　　　　　　　　　　—Tim Ferriss, bestselling author of
　　　　　　　　　　　The 4-Hour Workweek

"A worthy read for business types.... Hsieh is a fun narrator to hang out with for a few hours."　　　　　　　—*New York Post*

"In this fascinating (and often hilarious) account, Tony explains how he turns his beliefs into actions that really do deliver happiness."
　　　　　　　　　　　—Gretchen Rubin, bestselling author of
　　　　　　　　　　　The Happiness Project

"DELIVERING HAPPINESS is relatable, practical, and intimate."
　　　　　　　　　　　—*Inc.* magazine

"This book could start a revolution."
　　　　　　　　　　　—Marshall Goldsmith, bestselling author of
　　　　　　　　　　　Mojo: How to Get It, How to Keep It,
　　　　　　　　　　　How to Get It Back If You Lose It

"Tony Hsieh is a wise guy. Sincerely. He's one of the wisest and most thoughtful business leaders of the modern age. This insightful book isn't just an enjoyable read. It's a wonderful instruction manual for how twenty-first-century companies create value and happiness at the same time.

—Chip Conley, founder and CEO of
Joie de Vivre Hospitality and author of
Peak: How Great Companies Get Their Mojo from Maslow

"This book illustrates so many of Zappos's core values: It's open and honest, passionate and humble, fun and a little weird. Even if you don't care about business, technology, or shoes, you'll be drawn in by this American tale of how hard work, laziness, talent, and failure blend together to create an extraordinary life. You'll learn a lot about happiness along the way, too. I loved it."

—Jonathan Haidt, professor of psychology,
University of Virginia, and author of
The Happiness Hypothesis

"A glimpse into the mind of one of the most remarkable business leaders of our time...Like its author, the book is authentic, oddly original, doesn't take itself too seriously—yet delivers a potent message. Weaving together history, personal philosophy, and insights from one of the most intriguing companies in world, DELIVERING HAPPINESS works on the mind, the heart, and the soul. This book needs to be read by anyone who takes the happiness of other people seriously."

—Dave Logan, professor, Marshall School of
Business/University of Southern California,
and coauthor of *Tribal Leadership* and
The Three Laws of Performance

DELIVERING
Happiness

A PATH TO PROFITS, PASSION, AND PURPOSE

TONY HSIEH

GRAND CENTRAL
PUBLISHING

NEW YORK BOSTON

Grand Central Publishing
Hachette Book Group
1290 Avenue of the Americas
New York, NY 10104

www.HachetteBookGroup.com

Printed in the United States of America

RRD-C

Originally published in hardcover by Hachette Book Group.

First trade edition: March 2013
10 9 8 7 6 5 4 3

Grand Central Publishing is a division of Hachette Book Group, Inc.
The Grand Central Publishing name and logo are trademarks of Hachette Book Group, Inc.

The Hachette Speakers Bureau provides a wide range of authors for speaking events. To find out more, go to www.hachettespeakersbureau.com or call (866) 376-6591.

The publisher is not responsible for websites (or their content) that are not owned by the publisher.

The Library of Congress has cataloged the hardcover edition as follows:

Hsieh, Tony.
    Delivering happiness : a path to profits, passion, and purpose / Tony Hsieh. — 1st ed.
    p. cm.
    Includes index.
    ISBN 978-0-446-56304-8
    1. Success in business. 2. Leadership. I. Title.
    HF5386.H864 2010
    658.4'09—dc22

                                2009047113

ISBN 978-0-446-57622-2 (pbk.)

This book is dedicated to Ava Zech and all of the other aspiring entrepreneurs and business leaders of tomorrow. Happy eleventh birthday, Ava!

Contents

Preface   *xiii*

Introduction: Finding My Way   *1*

SECTION I

PROFITS

1. In Search of Profits   5
2. You Win Some, You Lose Some   30
3. Diversify   55

SECTION II

PROFITS AND PASSION

4. Concentrate Your Position   93
5. Platform for Growth: Brand, Culture, Pipeline   130

SECTION III

PROFITS, PASSION, AND PURPOSE

6. Taking It to the Next Level 203
7. End Game 228

Epilogue 243
Appendix: Online Resources 245
Index 247

*There's a difference between knowing the path
and walking the path.*
—MORPHEUS, *THE MATRIX*

Preface

I've been an entrepreneur for most of my life. I think it's because I've always enjoyed being creative and experimenting, applying lessons that I've learned along the way to both new ventures and my personal life.

In 1996, I co-founded LinkExchange, which was sold to Microsoft in 1998 for $265 million.

In 1999, I got involved with Zappos as an adviser and investor, and eventually became CEO. We grew the company from almost no sales in 1999 to over $1 billion in gross merchandise sales, annually.

In 2009, Zappos was acquired by Amazon in a deal valued at over $1.2 billion on the day of closing.

From an outsider's perspective, both companies may have seemed like overnight successes, but there were a lot of mistakes made and a lot of lessons learned along the way. Many of my philosophies and approaches were actually shaped by my experiences growing up.

I've also always been an avid book reader. At Zappos, we encourage our employees to read books from our library to help them grow, both personally and professionally. There are many books that have influenced our thinking at Zappos and helped us get to where we are today.

I decided to write this book to help people avoid making many of the same mistakes that I've made. I also hope that this book will serve as encouragement to established businesses as well as entrepreneurs who want to defy conventional wisdom and create their own paths to success.

How This Book Is Structured

This book is divided into three sections.

The first section is titled "Profits" and consists mostly of stories of me growing up and eventually finding my way to Zappos. Some of the stories are about my early adventures as an entrepreneur, while others are about a younger version of me rebelling against what was expected.

The second section, "Profits and Passion," is more business-oriented, covering many of the important philosophies that we believe in and live by at Zappos. I also share some of the internal e-mails and documents that we continue to use to this day.

The third section is titled "Profits, Passion, and Purpose." It outlines our vision at Zappos for taking things to the next level, and will hopefully challenge you to do the same.

This book is not meant to be a comprehensive corporate history of Zappos or any of the previous businesses I've been involved in. It's also not meant to be a complete autobiography. As such, I haven't mentioned everyone who contributed or played a role in my life. (If I had, there would have been way too many names for readers to try to keep track of and remember.) The purpose of this book is to give some of the highlights of the path that I took in my journey toward discovering how to find happiness in business and in life.

Finally, as you read through this book, you'll probably notice some sentences that aren't the best examples of English grammar. Except where third-party contributions to the book are specifically noted, I wrote this book without the use of a ghostwriter. I'm not a professional writer, and in many cases I purposely chose to do things that would probably make my high school English teachers cringe, such as ending a sentence with a preposition. I did this partly because I wanted the writing to reflect how I would normally talk, and partly just to annoy all my high school English teachers (who I appreciate dearly).

Although I did not use a ghostwriter, many people helped out behind the scenes with feedback, suggestions, and encouragement, and I'm grateful for everyone's involvement. There isn't enough room to list everyone who contributed, but I would like to specifically thank Jenn Lim, my long-time friend and backup brain. She acted as project manager and organizer of the entire book-writing process, and she was key to seeing this book from inception to finish. She also collected and helped edit many of the third-party contributions, some of which are in this book, and many more of which are available on the Web site at www.deliveringhappinessbook.com.

Introduction:
Finding My Way

Wow, I thought to myself.

The room was packed. I was on stage at our all-hands meeting, looking over a crowd of seven hundred Zappos employees who were standing up cheering and clapping. A lot of them even had tears of happiness streaming down their faces.

Forty-eight hours ago, we had announced to the world that Amazon was acquiring us. To the rest of the world, it was all about the money. The headlines from the press said things like "Amazon Buys Zappos for Close to $1 Billion," "Largest Acquisition in Amazon's History," and "What Everyone Made from the Zappos Sale."

In November 1998, LinkExchange, the company that I'd co-founded, was sold to Microsoft for $265 million after two and a half years. Now, in July 2009, as CEO of Zappos, I had just announced that Amazon was acquiring Zappos right after we had celebrated our ten-year anniversary. (The acquisition would officially close a few months later in a stock and cash transaction, with the shares valued at $1.2 billion on the day of closing.) In both scenarios, the deals looked similar: They both worked out to about $100 million per year. From the outside, this looked like history repeating itself, just at a larger scale.

Nothing could be further from the truth.

To all of us in the room, we knew it wasn't just about the

money. Together, we had built a business that combined profits, passion, and purpose. And we knew that it wasn't just about building a business. It was about building a lifestyle that was about delivering happiness to everyone, including ourselves.

Time stood still during that moment on stage. The unified energy and emotion of everyone in the room was reminiscent of when I'd attended my first rave ten years earlier, where I'd witnessed thousands of people dancing in unison, with everyone feeding off of each other's energy. Back then, the rave community came together based on their four core values known as PLUR: Peace, Love, Unity, Respect.

At Zappos, we had collectively come up with our own set of ten core values. Those values bonded us together, and were an important part of the path that led us to this moment.

Looking over the crowd, I realized that every person took a different path to get here, but our paths somehow all managed to intersect with one another here and now. I realized that for me, the path that got me here began long before Zappos, and long before LinkExchange. I thought about all the different businesses I had been a part of, all the people who had been in my life, and all the adventures I had been on. I thought about mistakes that I had made and lessons that I had learned. I started thinking back to college, then back to high school, then back to middle school, and then back to elementary school.

As all the eyes in the room were on me, I tried to trace back to where my path had begun. In my mind, I was traveling backward in time searching for the answer. Although I was pretty sure I wasn't dying, my life was flashing before my eyes. I was obsessed with figuring it out, and I knew I had to do it this very moment, before the energy in the room dissipated, before time stopped standing still. I didn't know why. I just knew I *needed* to know where my path began.

And then, right before reality returned and time started moving again, I figured it out.

My path began on a worm farm.

PROFITS

1

In Search of Profits

Worm Farm

First, they ignore you, then they laugh at you,
then they fight you, then you win.
—GANDHI

I'm pretty sure that Gandhi had no idea who I was when I was nine years old. And I'm pretty sure I had no idea who he was either. But if Gandhi had known about my vision and childhood dream of making lots and lots of money by breeding and selling earthworms in mass quantities to the public, I think he might have used the same quote to inspire me to become the number one worm seller in the world.

Unfortunately, Gandhi didn't stop by my home to offer me his sage advice and wisdom. Instead, on my ninth birthday, I told my parents that I wanted them to drive me an hour north of our house to Sonoma, to a place that was currently the number one worm seller in the county. Little did they know that I was conspiring to be their biggest competitor.

My parents paid $33.45 for a box of mud that was guaranteed to contain at least one hundred earthworms. I remember I had read in a book that you could cut a worm in half and both halves would regrow themselves. That sounded really cool, but seemed like a lot of work, so I went through with a better plan instead: I built a "worm box" in my backyard, which was basically like a sandbox with chicken wire on the bottom. Instead of filling it with sand, I filled it with mud and spread the hundred-plus earthworms around so they could slither freely and make lots of little baby earthworms.

Every day, I would take a few raw egg yolks and dump them on top of my worm farm. I was pretty confident that this would cause the worms to reproduce more quickly, as I had heard that some professional athletes drink raw eggs for breakfast. My parents were pretty confident that selling worms would not bring me the riches that I was dreaming of, but they allowed me to continue to feed the worms with raw egg yolks every day. I think the only reason they allowed me to do this was because of the high cholesterol content of the egg yolks. If the worms were eating the egg yolks, then that meant that my brothers and I were only eating the low-cholesterol egg whites. My mom was always making sure we weren't eating things that might raise our cholesterol levels. I think maybe she saw a segment on the local news about cholesterol that freaked her out one night.

After thirty days of putting the worms on the raw-egg-yolk diet, I decided to check on their progress, so I dug through the mud in the worm farm to see if any baby earthworms had been born yet. Unfortunately, I didn't find any baby earthworms. Even more problematically, I didn't find any adult earthworms either. I spent an hour carefully sifting through all the mud that was in my worm box. Every single worm was gone. They had apparently escaped through the chicken wire that was at the bottom of the worm box. Or had been eaten by birds that were attracted to the raw egg yolks.

My burgeoning worm empire was officially out of business. I told my parents that being a worm farmer was kind of boring anyway, but the truth was that I felt bad about failing. If Thomas

Edison was still alive, he could have stopped by my house and encouraged me with his perspective on failure:

> *I failed my way to success.*
> —THOMAS EDISON

He was probably too busy working on other stuff, though, because, like Gandhi, he never did stop by my house. Maybe they were too busy hanging out with each other.

Growing Up

My mom and dad each emigrated from Taiwan to the United States in order to attend graduate school at the University of Illinois, where they met and got married. Although I was born in Illinois, my only memories of that period of my life were jumping off a diving board that was twelve feet high and catching fireflies. Early memories are always a blur, but I believe those were actually two separate memories, as I find it unlikely that as a two-year-old I would have been able to actually catch a firefly while in midair.

When I was five years old, my dad got a job in California, so we all moved to Marin County, which is across the Golden Gate Bridge, just north of San Francisco. We lived in Lucas Valley. Our house was about a twenty-minute drive from Skywalker Ranch, where George Lucas (of *Star Wars* fame) lived and ran his movie business from.

My parents were your typical Asian American parents. My dad was a chemical engineer for Chevron, and my mom was a social worker. They had high expectations in terms of academic performance for myself as well as for my two younger brothers. Andy was two years younger than me, and four years after moving to California, my youngest brother David was born.

There weren't a lot of Asian families living in Marin County, but somehow my parents managed to find all ten of them, and we would have regular gatherings where all the parents and kids would get together for a potluck and hang out afterward. The kids would watch TV while the adults were in a separate room socializing and bragging to each other about their kids' accomplishments. That was just part of the Asian culture: The accomplishments of the children were the trophies that many parents defined their own success and status by. We were the ultimate scorecard.

There were three categories of accomplishments that mattered to the Asian parents.

Category 1 was academic accomplishments: Getting good grades, any type of award or public recognition, getting good SAT scores, or being part of the school's math team counted toward this. The most important part of all of this was which college your child ended up attending. Harvard yielded the most prestigious bragging rights.

Category 2 was career accomplishments: Becoming a medical doctor or getting a PhD was seen as the ultimate accomplishment, because in both cases it meant that you could go from being "Mr. Hsieh" to "Dr. Hsieh."

Category 3 was musical instrument mastery: Almost every Asian child was forced to learn either piano or violin or both, and at each of the gatherings, the children had to perform in front of the group of parents after dinner was over. This was ostensibly to entertain the parents, but really it was a way for parents to compare their kids with each other.

My parents, just like the other Asian parents, were pretty strict in raising me so that we could win in all three categories. I was only allowed to watch one hour of TV every week. I was expected to get straight A's in all my classes, and my parents had me take practice SAT tests throughout all of middle school and high school. The SAT is a standardized test that is typically only taken once, toward the end of high school, as part of the college application process. But my parents wanted me to start preparing for it when I was in sixth grade.

In middle school, I ended up playing four different musical instruments: piano, violin, trumpet, and French horn. During the school year, I was supposed to practice each of them for thirty minutes every day if it was a weekday, and an hour per instrument on Saturdays and Sundays. During the summer, it was an hour per instrument per day, which I believe should be classified as a form of cruel and unusual punishment for kids who want to experience the *vacation* part of *summer vacation*.

So I figured out a way to still enjoy my weekends and summer vacations. I would wake up early at 6:00 AM, while my parents were still sleeping, and go downstairs to where the piano was. Instead of actually playing the piano, I would use a tape recorder and play back an hour-long session that I had recorded earlier. Then, at 7:00 AM, I would go up to my room, lock the door, and replay an hour-long recording of me playing the violin. I spent the time reading a book or *Boys' Life* magazine instead.

As you can imagine, my piano and violin teachers could not understand why I showed no improvement every time they saw me during my weekly lessons. I think they just thought I was a slow learner. From my perspective, I just couldn't see how learning how to play all these musical instruments would result in any type of benefit that was scalable.

(Hopefully my mom won't get too mad when she reads this. I should probably pay her back for all the money she spent on my piano and violin lessons.)

My parents, especially my mom, had high hopes that I would eventually go to medical school or get a PhD. They believed that formalized education was the most important thing, but to me, having the first twenty-five years of my life already mapped out seemed too regimented and stifling.

I was much more interested in running my own business and figuring out different ways to make money. When I was growing up, my parents always told me not to worry about making money so that I could focus on my academics. They told me they would pay for all my education until I got my MD or PhD. They also told me they would buy whatever clothes I wanted. Luckily for them, I never had any fashion sense, so I never asked for much.

I always fantasized about making money, because to me, money meant that later on in life I would have the freedom to do whatever I wanted. The idea of one day running my own company also meant that I could be creative and eventually live life on my own terms.

I did a lot of garage sales during my elementary school years. When I ran out of junk from my parents' garage to sell, I asked a friend if we could hold a garage sale at her house. We put all of the junk from her parents' house on display out in the driveway, made some lemonade, and then dressed her in a little girl's outfit that made her look five years younger. The idea was that even if people didn't buy anything, we could at least sell them some lemonade. We ended up making more money selling lemonade than anything else from the garage sale.

In middle school, I looked for other ways to make money. I had a newspaper route, but I soon discovered that being an independent contractor delivering newspapers on my bike was really just a way for the local newspaper to get around child labor laws. After doing the math, I figured out that my pay worked out to about $2 per hour.

I quit my paper route and decided to make my own newsletter instead. Each issue contained about twenty pages of stories I wrote, word puzzles, and jokes. I printed my newsletter on bright orange paper, named it *The Gobbler,* and priced it at $5 each. I sold four copies to my friends in middle school. I figured I either needed to make more friends who could afford to buy my newsletter, or needed to figure out another revenue stream. So when I got my next haircut, I showed my barber a copy of *The Gobbler* and asked him if he wanted to buy a full-page ad in the next issue for $20.

When he said yes, I knew I was on to something. All I needed to do was to sell four more ads and I would make $100, which was more money than I had ever seen in my life. Full of confidence after my first sale, I went to the businesses that were next door to the barber and asked if they wanted to advertise in what was sure to be the next newsletter sensation to sweep the country, or at least the county.

Everyone said no, but they said it in the most polite way possible. A few weeks later, I put out the second issue of *The Gobbler*. This time, I only sold two copies.

I decided to discontinue operations.

It was too much work and my friends were running out of their lunch money.

My brother Andy and I used to look forward to every issue of *Boys' Life* magazine each month and read it cover-to-cover. My favorite section was at the very back—a classified ads section for ordering fantastic things that I never even knew existed but knew I had to have one day. There were all sorts of magic tricks and novelty items (for the longest time, I thought the definition of *novelty* was "really, really cool"), including a kit for converting a vacuum cleaner into a mini hovercraft.

But what interested me the most was the full-page ad on the back of the magazine, which showed all sorts of prizes you could earn by selling greeting cards. It seemed so easy: just go around the neighborhood door-to-door, sell some Christmas cards (which *everyone* needed, the ad assured me), earn lots of points, and redeem the points for that skateboard or toy I never had but now wanted.

So I decided to order some sample greeting cards and a catalog, which arrived within a week. I was still on summer vacation, so I had plenty of time to go door-to-door. My first stop was my next-door neighbor's house.

I showed the woman who answered the door the catalog of all

the different varieties of Christmas cards. She told me that since it was still August, they weren't really in the market for Christmas cards just yet. I thought she had a valid point. I felt stupid trying to sell Christmas cards in August, so that also ended up being my last stop.

I went back home to try to think of a business idea that had less seasonality to it.

In elementary school, I had a best friend named Gustav. We used to do everything together, hanging out at each other's houses, putting on plays for our parents to watch, teaching each other secret languages and codes, and having sleepovers once a week.

During one of my visits to his house, he let me borrow a book called *Free Stuff for Kids*. It was the greatest book ever. Inside were hundreds of offers for free and up-to-a-dollar items that kids could order, including things like free maps, 50-cent pens, free bumper stickers, and free samples of products. For each item, all you had to do was write a letter to each of the different mailing addresses, including a SASE (which I learned was short for "self-addressed stamped envelope") and whatever up-to-a-dollar payment they were asking for, if any. Gustav and I went through the book and ordered all the items that we thought were cool.

After my ten-minute stint as a door-to-door Christmas greeting card salesman, I went back home to read through the classifieds section of *Boys' Life* again and saw an ad for a button-making kit for $50. The kit allowed you to convert any photo or piece of paper into a pin-on button that you could then wear on your shirt. The cost of the parts to make the button was 25 cents per button.

I went to my bookshelf and grabbed the book I had borrowed from Gustav years earlier and never returned, and looked through it to see if any of the companies in the book were already offering photo pin-on buttons. There weren't any.

Excited, I typed up a letter to the publisher of the book and pretended that I was already in the button-making business and wanted to be considered for inclusion in next year's issue of the book. In order to look even more like I was running a legitimate business, I added "Dept. FSFK" as part of my mailing address. *FSFK* was my secret code for "Free Stuff For Kids." My offer was for kids to send in a photo, a SASE, and $1. I would turn it into a pin-on button, and then send it back in the SASE. My profit would be 75 cents per order.

A couple of months later, I received a letter back from the publisher. They said my offer had been selected to be included in the next edition of the book. I told my parents I had to order the $50 button-making kit, plus spend another $50 for parts, but that I would pay them back after my first hundred orders.

I don't think my parents thought I would actually get a hundred orders. They had heard me talk before about how much money I would make selling a hundred copies of *The Gobbler*, or how much I would get from getting a hundred orders of greeting cards. But I was still getting good grades in school, so I think they thought of allowing me to order the button-making kit and parts as more of a reward for that.

A couple of months later, I got a copy of the new edition of the book. It was pretty cool to see my home address in print, in a real book. I showed the book to my parents, and anxiously waited for the first order to come in.

The mailman for our neighborhood always went on the same route to deliver mail. Our house was near the bottom of a hill, and he would start his route at the bottom on the opposite side of the street, go up the hill, turn around, and then come back down the hill. So anytime I heard the mail truck on the opposite side of the street, I knew the mail would be delivered exactly twelve minutes later to our house, and I would wait outside the house for him to arrive. Usually this would happen at around 1:36 PM.

Two weeks after the book was published, I received my first order. I opened the envelope, and inside was a picture of a twelve-year-old girl in a red plaid dress holding a French poodle. More importantly, there was a dollar bill inside. I was officially in business! I turned the photo into a button and sent it back in the self-addressed stamped envelope. Later that evening, I told my parents about it. I think they were a little surprised I got even a single order. I gave them the dollar bill, and recorded in my journal that my outstanding debt had been reduced to $99.

The next day, I got two orders. Business had doubled overnight. And over the next month, there were days when I would get ten orders in a single day. By the end of the first month, I had made over $200. I had paid down all my outstanding debt, and was making pretty good money for a kid in middle school. But making the buttons was taking up to an hour a day. On days when I had a lot of homework, I wouldn't have time to make the buttons, so sometimes I would let the orders pile up until the weekend. Over the weekend, I'd have to spend four or five hours making buttons. The money was great, but having to stay indoors on weekends was not, so I decided it was time to upgrade to a $300 semi-automated button machine in order to improve my efficiency and productivity.

My button business brought in a steady $200 a month during my middle school years. I think the biggest lesson I learned was that it was possible to run a successful business by mail order, without any face-to-face interaction.

Occasionally, when I was too busy, I would outsource some of the labor to my brothers. By the time I graduated from middle school, I'd started to get bored with making buttons every day, so I decided to pass the business on to my brother Andy. My thought was that eventually I would start another mail-order business that I was more passionate about.

I didn't know it at the time, but the button business was going to become a family enterprise. A few years later, Andy passed the business on to our youngest brother David. And a few years after that, we stopped advertising in the book and shut down the business. My dad had gotten a promotion that required him to move to Hong Kong, and he brought my mom and my brother

David along with him. There were no more siblings to pass the business on to.

Looking back, I think we should have had a better succession plan.

Dialing for Dollars

I remember thinking that the first day of high school really didn't feel that different from the last day of middle school. I guess in my head I had thought that suddenly I would feel older and more mature, that somehow life would suddenly be different now that I was in high school.

One day, while wandering around the school library, I discovered the computer lab that was hidden off to the side of the library. I met the computer science teacher, Ms. Gore, who suggested that I sign up for her Pascal class. I had never heard of Pascal before. She told me it was a computer programming language and taking the class would prepare me for a national AP computer science test. I didn't know what an AP test was, except that it was something that would look good on my college application. In middle school, I had learned to do some BASIC computer programming on my own and enjoyed it, so I decided to sign up for Pascal.

I enjoyed taking the class, and ended up spending my lunch hours and after-school hours in the computer lab. I didn't know it at the time, but two years later, I would be teaching the Pascal class there for summer school. There were a few other people who were regulars in the lab as well, and we ended up spending a lot of time together.

We were introduced to the world of BBSs. I learned that *BBS* was an acronym for "Bulletin Board System." One of the computers in the lab had a modem attached to it, which was a special device that connected to a regular phone line. With the modem, the computer had the ability to call other computers and talk to them.

We had a list of phone numbers for the different BBSs that

were local calls for us, and we would call up each of the BBSs and connect to the electronic equivalent of a community cork bulletin board that students used in the reception area downstairs: Anyone could leave a message, post an ad, start a discussion, download files, or join in on a debate on a wide range of topics. It was the pre-Internet version of Craigslist.

We soon discovered that the computer and phone line were not limited to just local calls, so we started making long-distance calls to BBSs all across the country. It was amazing being able to join in discussions with strangers from Seattle, New York, and Miami. We suddenly had access to an entire world that we didn't know existed before.

One day during lunch, when Ms. Gore was out of the lab on her lunch break, someone came up with the idea of unplugging the modem from the wall jack and plugging a regular telephone in there instead. We weren't sure if it would actually work or not, but when we picked up the handset of the phone, we heard a dial tone. We now had the ability to make any phone call we wanted to for free. We just didn't know who we should call with our newfound secret power.

I asked if anyone had heard of 976 numbers. I had seen all sorts of ads on TV for different 976 numbers. You could call 976-JOKE, for example, to hear the joke of the day, at the cost of 99 cents a call. So we tried calling 976-JOKE, and heard a joke that wasn't very funny. We tried calling the number again to try to get a better joke, and all they did was replay the same one. In retrospect, I guess it made sense since it was supposed to be the joke of the day, not the joke of the minute.

Then we started just trying to dial random 976 numbers to see what we would get. One of the numbers we tried was 976-SEXY. It started out with an automated recording saying that the charge would be $2.99 per minute and that the service was for adults only. I was told by the recording that if I was under twenty-one, then I should hang up immediately.

So of course I didn't hang up. My curiosity was piqued.

A woman answered the phone and started talking to me in a sultry voice. "Hi there," she said. "Are you feeling sexy right now?"

Well, this certainly seemed to be a lot more interesting and fun than connecting through the computer to other BBSers in New York. A whole new world was indeed opening up to me.

"Um. Yes," I said in my deepest voice possible.

Suddenly, the sultry voice became a regular, annoyed voice, reminiscent of my geometry teacher disciplining me for showing up late to class.

"Are you over twenty-one?" she asked suspiciously. Apparently my deepest voice was not actually that deep. Puberty can be such an awkward stage in one's life.

I took a deep breath. "Yes, of course," I said confidently.

"Okay then, what year were you born?"

I was caught completely off guard. Apparently I couldn't do math in my head fast enough to fool her. The jig was up.

"Twenty-one years ago!" I shouted and quickly hung up the phone. My friends and I started laughing uncontrollably. After a few minutes, we did the calculations and we all practiced saying with confidence that we were born in 1966. We wanted to make sure we didn't make the same mistake again in the future.

Over the next few weeks, a small group of us would gather on a daily basis in the computer lab during lunch and take turns calling 976-SEXY. We could only call during lunch hour because that was the only time Ms. Gore wasn't also in the room. We were part of a secret club, and the first rule of computer-lab-lunch club was that you did not talk about computer-lab-lunch club.

Nobody had any clue what we were up to.

And then one day, as we all gathered during lunch hour, we were surprised that Ms. Gore hadn't left to go to lunch yet. Maybe she had some work to finish up first, so we decided to use the computer to call up BBSs while waiting for her to leave.

"Hey guys?" Ms. Gore asked. We all looked up at her. "Have

any of you been making phone calls to 976-7399? I just got this phone bill and it says that in the past month, over three hundred phone calls were made from the modem to that number. I just tried calling the number and it's not a computer answering."

We all looked at each other and then looked at her. I'm pretty sure we all looked guilty as could be, but we all remembered the first rule of computer-lab-lunch club, so we just looked at her and shrugged as innocently as we could.

"It must be some sort of mistake," Ms. Gore concluded. "I'll call the phone company and get them to remove all the charges. I don't think it's even humanly possible to make that many phone calls." Little did she know of our superhuman abilities.

And that was the end of computer-lab-lunch club.

Classic Economics

Computer lab shenanigans aside, I tried to expose myself to as many interesting things in high school as possible. My thought was that the more perspectives I could gain, the better.

I took a lot of foreign-language classes, including French, Spanish, Japanese, and even Latin. For my PE (physical education) requirement, instead of a more traditional sport, I decided to learn fencing (although truth be told, part of the appeal was that fencing class was only once a week). I took a jazz piano class to satisfy our music requirement, and a life drawing class to fulfill the art requirement. I joined the chess club and the electronics club, where I learned Morse code and became a certified ham radio operator.

To fulfill the community service requirement, I volunteered to work at a local theater and help convert it to a giant haunted house. During the week before Halloween, I volunteered as a tour guide. Each visitor donated $15 for a twenty-minute haunted house tour.

I really enjoyed being involved with theater, especially behind the scenes. I was the light board operator for many of our high school performances, and at one point even performed a magic act on stage with a friend for one of our talent shows. One of my first paying jobs in high school was operating the spotlight (known as a "follow spot" in theater lingo) for one of our local community theaters. There was something alluring about being involved in something where the sole purpose was to create an experience and emotional journey for people, and then to have nothing but memories left afterward to hold on to.

The regimen of having a fixed class schedule and doing homework started wearing on me though, so I started choosing classes based on how it affected my schedule rather than the class itself. One year, I managed to schedule my classes so that I only had one class to attend on Tuesdays, and then had the rest of the day off. I started making deals with my teachers in which they agreed to let me not attend their classes as long as I did well on their tests.

As for homework, I tried my best to find creative ways around actually doing any hard work. For Shakespeare class, one of our assignments was to write a sonnet. A sonnet is a fourteen-line poem written in iambic pentameter, meaning each line would alternate in a repeated pattern of unstressed and stressed syllables, while adhering to certain rhyming patterns. It all seemed way too complicated for me, so I decided to just submit fourteen lines of Morse code instead, where the entire poem was nothing but alternating dots and dashes.

Depending on the teacher's mood, I knew I was either going to get an A or an F. Luckily, my teacher decided to give me an "A+++++++++++." I think that's when I learned that, even in school, it sometimes pays to take risks and think outside the box.

One of my unhappier moments in high school was when I was accused of stealing someone's lunch card, which was the equivalent of a credit card for our cafeteria. I'm not sure exactly how someone's lunch card wound up in my pocket. My best guess is that the cashier probably handed me back someone's lunch card by accident on the previous day. In any case, I wound up before the Judicial Council, which was like a mini jury consisting of the school president and some members of the faculty.

I was given the opportunity to present my case, but I didn't really have a case because I had no idea how the lunch card wound up in my pocket. Instead, I went into the session with the blind faith that the right thing would happen as long as I told the truth, so that's exactly what I did. As it turned out, nobody believed me, and I was suspended from school for a day, which went on my official school record. I had done time for a crime I didn't commit.

I walked away from that experience with the lesson that sometimes the truth alone isn't enough, and that presentation of the truth was just as important as the truth. Ironically, our school's motto was "Truth is beauty, beauty truth," based on the John Keats's poem "Ode on a Grecian Urn."

I didn't feel very beautiful that day.

Apart from school-related activities, my biggest focus during high school was trying to figure out how I could make more money. I was hired as a video game tester for Lucasfilm. I got paid $6 an hour to play the *Indiana Jones and the Last Crusade* video game. It was a fun job, but it only paid $6 an hour, so when a higher-paying job came up, I took it right away.

By my senior year in high school, I had worked my way up to a computer programming job at a company called GDI. The job paid $15 per hour, which was pretty good money for a high school student. The actual work involved creating software that enabled government agencies and small businesses to fill out forms by computer instead of by paper.

To keep myself entertained, I would occasionally play pranks on my boss, who was an older French man with silver hair and a thick accent. He enjoyed drinking tea, and he had a regular routine of putting a cup of water in the microwave that was next to my desk, turning on the microwave, then going back to his office because he didn't want to wait around for the three minutes it took to heat up the water. Then he would return later and make his tea.

One time, I decided to turn off the microwave as soon as he left. When my boss returned a few minutes later, he noticed the water was still cold, so he thought that he had forgotten to turn it on. He set it to three minutes again and left.

As soon as he was out of sight, I turned off the microwave again. When he returned the second time, he noticed that the water was cold yet again, and muttered something about the microwave being broken. I did my best to not crack a smile.

He decided to try to heat his water one last time, except this time he set the microwave for five minutes just to be sure, and he walked away a bit perplexed and frustrated.

When he finally returned, he opened the microwave door and yelled "What is this?!" Then he started laughing. He looked around the office and saw the guilt on all of our faces, because everyone was in on the joke. He took out his teacup and showed everyone what I had done a few minutes earlier.

The teacup was full of ice cubes.

Everyone in the office started laughing uncontrollably. I don't think any of us had laughed that hard in a long time, and it was great to see how having a little fun in the office could lighten everyone's mood.

I'm also glad that I didn't get fired that day.

While the money that I was making at GDI was good, I kept thinking back to the days of my button-making mail-order business and the excitement and anticipation of waiting for the mailman to show up at my house. I thought about how the company that sold me the button-making kit must have been itself a successful mail-order business, because I had ordered from the classifieds section at the back of *Boys' Life* magazine.

So I decided that I should try selling something there as well. Since I'd been reading some magic books in my spare time, I came up with the idea of selling a magic trick, in which a coin would appear to dissolve through a piece of rubber. It was actually a pretty cool trick. Everyone I had shown the trick to had been amazed by it and wanted to know how it was done. Aside from a coin, a cup, and a rubber band, the only other thing required to do the trick was a latex square, which I learned was the same thing that dentists use and refer to as a "dental dam."

I did some research and found that if I bought in large-enough quantities, I could purchase dental dams at less than 20 cents apiece. A classified ad in the back of *Boys' Life* cost $800, so if I priced the magic trick at $10, then I would almost break even if I got just eighty orders.

It seemed almost too easy. My button-making business had been pulling in two to three hundred orders a month. I assumed *Boys' Life* had a much wider readership than *Free Stuff for Kids*. Plus, this magic trick was much cooler than a photo button. At two hundred orders, the cost of my supplies would have been $40, so I would make a profit of $1,160. At three hundred orders, my profit would be $2,140. I had discovered the beauty of selling products with high average selling prices and high gross margins.

The $800 I paid to *Boys' Life* for the classified ad was almost two weeks' worth of pay, but I viewed it as an investment. Due to the long lead time for my ad to appear in print, it would take a couple of months for the orders to start coming in, but I was patient and thinking about the long term.

After what seemed like an eternity, the mailman finally showed up with the issue of *Boys' Life* that my classified ad was in. It was great placement, and a week later I received my first order. It seemed like the easiest $10 I had ever made, and I eagerly waited for my next order to arrive.

Except that day never came.

That one order was the only order I ever got for my mail-order magic trick business. From my button-making success, I'd thought that I was the invincible king of mail order, when all that had happened was that I had gotten lucky.

I learned a valuable lesson in humility. And somewhat ironically, I'd just learned the term *hubris* in my Greek history class, which was defined as "an exaggerated sense of pride or self-confidence," and it caused the downfall of many a Greek hero.

I also learned that it was pretty painful to bet the farm on something that didn't work out. Now that I think about it, I hadn't just bet the farm.

Eight hundred dollars was actually the equivalent of twenty-four worm farms.

College

For college, I applied to Brown, UC Berkeley, Stanford, MIT, Princeton, Cornell, Yale, and Harvard. I got into all of them. My first choice was Brown, because it had an advertising major, which seemed like it could be more relevant to the business world than any of the other majors offered by the other colleges.

My parents, however, wanted me to go to Harvard because that was the most prestigious, especially among the Asian community, so that's where I ended up going.

The first thing I bought when I got to Harvard was a TV. I was no longer restricted to watching one hour of TV per week by my parents, so I was watching four hours of TV a day in my newfound freedom. I found out that while I was spending my time watching TV, some other students in my dorm were busy playing practical jokes, like removing all the toilet paper from the girls' bathroom or turning our proctor's bathtub into a giant vat of hot tea (our proctor was not amused).

I arranged my schedule so that I only had classes from 9:00 AM to 1:00 PM on Mondays, Wednesdays, and Fridays, leaving my Tuesdays and Thursdays completely free. This sounded like a great idea in theory, but being a night owl, I ended up on a strange forty-eight-hour schedule, where I would stay up for thirty-two hours in a row and then sleep for sixteen hours straight.

On class days, my 8:00 AM alarm was the most unwelcome sound in the world. I would hit the snooze button repeatedly, and then tell myself that I could skip the first class of the day and get the notes from someone else later. Then, an hour later, I would convince myself that since that logic worked so well for the first class, I could apply it to the second class, so I missed that class as well. By the time I was supposed to be getting ready to go to my third class, I reasoned that I had already skipped two classes, so one more class really wasn't that big a deal. And finally, by the time I was supposed to be headed to my last class of the day, I figured there was no point in only attending one class when I had skipped all the others. The incremental benefit from getting up just to go to that one class just didn't seem worth it.

So, basically, I ended up not attending any of my classes freshman year. Since I never made it out of bed in the first place, I was too lazy to shower and walk all the way over to the lunch hall. I ended up eating a lot of ramen during the day and watching every episode of *Days of Our Lives*.

My freshman year was spent mostly hanging out with friends I'd made who lived in the same dorm, which was called Canaday A. We watched a lot of TV together, played video games, and talked a lot. Inspired by my *Gobbler* days, I created the *Canaday A Newsletter*. There was a core group of about fifteen of us, and we were inseparable. Most of us never made any friends outside of our core group, and we managed to stick together during all four years of college.

Just like in high school, I tried to do the least amount of work in college while still getting decent grades. I took classes like American Sign Language, linguistics, and Mandarin Chinese (which I already spoke with my parents). To fulfill one of my core requirements, I enrolled in a class on the Bible. The good news about the class was that there never was really any homework that I had to turn in and be graded on, so I ended up never going to the class. The bad news was that my grade in the class was going to be based on what I got on the final exam, which I was completely unprepared for, since I had never opened up any of the textbooks we were supposed to have been reading throughout the semester. I think the skill I honed the most in college was procrastination.

Two weeks before the final exam for the class, the professor passed out a list of the hundred possible topics we would be tested on. We were told that, for the actual exam, five of those topics would be chosen randomly, and we'd each have to write a few paragraphs about each of those five topics.

There was no way I could do all the reading in two weeks that I was supposed to have been doing throughout the semester, and I wasn't too keen on flunking out of the class either.

They say that necessity is the mother of invention. At Harvard, we could use our computers to log on to electronic newsgroups, which were the equivalent of the BBSs that I had played around with in high school. I posted a message to one of the electronic newsgroups and invited all the Harvard students who were taking the Bible class to participate in the largest study group that had ever been created, because this one would be virtual.

For anyone who was interested, I would assign them three out of the possible hundred topics to research thoroughly. Each student then had to e-mail me their paragraphs on each of those three topics as if they were the actual topics chosen for the final exam. I would compile everyone's responses together, have them photocopied and bound, and then distribute the binders for $20 each. You were only allowed to buy a binder if you had contributed your three topics to the project.

As it turned out, there was a lot of interest, so I actually received multiple answers for each topic from different people. Without ever opening up a book or doing any writing myself, I ended up with the most comprehensive study guide that had ever been created, and that everyone found useful. As a bonus, I also ended up making a little profit on the side. *The Crimson,* our school newspaper, wrote a story about the whole virtual study group experiment, and I ended up doing fine on the final exam.

I had discovered the power of crowdsourcing.

I was exposed to a lot of different things for the first time in college.

I joined the movie society, which made money by renting films to be shown in one of the school auditoriums, and then sold tickets to the students. I visited a friend's farm, where I learned how to milk cows during the day, and wound up getting stitches at night after I fell flat on my chin while attempting to learn how to ice skate. I'm not sure whether the cow-milking or the emergency-room stitching was more traumatic.

I won tickets on the local radio station to my first concert and got to see U2 perform during their Zoo TV tour. I held various jobs during school, including catering at weddings and bartending, after having completed a four-hour session at the Harvard Bartending School and earning a certificate in Mixology. I also held various computer programming jobs, including working for Harvard Student Agencies, Spinnaker Software, and a summer internship at Microsoft.

One of the companies I worked for was BBN, which developed the technology that eventually became the backbone of the Internet. BBN contracted with different government agencies, so I was required to get a background check in order for me to obtain Secret status, which was one level below Top Secret status. Apparently there were levels of government secrecy that were so high that even the name of the status was classified.

For most of my work at BBN, I had to go into a large, isolated room with multiple levels of security, including electronic badges and secret access codes through different doors. I wasn't allowed to bring anything into or out of the room, especially electronic devices or any type of electronic media or storage.

One summer, I decided to head across the river from Cambridge to Boston to explore the city. I somehow wandered past the headquarters of the Boston chapter of the Guardian Angels, a street gang whose mission was to prevent and fight crime. I ended up becoming a member for a few months and helped patrol the subway system and back alleys of Boston.

I was given the gang name of "Secret." At first, I thought it was because I had mentioned my Secret status with the government, but I learned later that one of the other gang members had originally wanted to name me "Ancient Chinese Secret."

During my junior and senior years in college, I realized that I missed running my own business, so I took over the Quincy House Grille, which was an eating area on the ground floor of the Quincy House dorm. Our dorm housed about three hundred students, and the Quincy House Grille was a late-night gathering spot for students to play foosball and pinball, and satisfy their late-night cravings.

One of my roommates, Sanjay, ran the grill with me. We were responsible for setting the menu and prices, ordering from suppliers, hiring employees, and occasionally making the food ourselves.

At the time, a city ordinance prevented fast-food establishments from opening up anywhere near campus, so I decided to take the subway to the next stop to the nearest McDonald's. I talked to the manager there and he sold me a hundred frozen McDonald's hamburger patties and buns, which I then loaded into a taxicab and brought back to our dorm. For a couple of months, this was part of my daily routine. Because there was no other place on campus to get McDonald's burgers, I was able to charge $3 for burgers that cost me $1 to buy.

I eventually got tired of making the daily runs to McDonald's, so I decided to see what it would take to turn the grill into a pizza business instead. I learned that pizzas were very high-margin. A large pizza cost less than $2 to make but could be sold for $10 (or more with additional toppings). And even more money could be made by selling pizzas by the slice. After some research, I discovered it would cost about $2,000 to invest in pizza ovens. It seemed like it was worth the risk, so I took a deep breath and wrote a check for $2,000.

I also wanted to make the grill more of a place where people wanted to hang out, so I spent many nights recording music videos from MTV onto videotape, pausing the recording anytime a commercial came on, because this was the pre-TiVo era. The videos playing in the background turned out to be a big hit, and combined with the new pizza offering, we ended up tripling sales at the grill compared with the previous year. The $2,000 investment was recouped within a couple of months.

It was through the pizza business that I met Alfred, who eventually would join Zappos as our CFO and COO. Alfred was actually my number one customer, and he stopped by every night to order a large pepperoni pizza from me.

We had two nicknames for Alfred while in college: "Human Trash Compactor" and "Monster." He earned these nicknames because every time a group of us would go out to a restaurant (usually it was a group of ten of us at a late-night greasy Chinese place called The Kong), he would literally finish everyone's leftovers from their plates. I was just thankful that I wasn't one of the roommates he shared his bathroom with.

So to me, it really wasn't that weird that Alfred would stop by every night to order an entire pepperoni pizza from me. But sometimes he would stop by a few hours later and order another large pepperoni pizza. At the time, I remember thinking to myself, *Wow, this boy can eat.*

I found out several years later that Alfred was taking the pizzas upstairs to his roommates, and then selling them off by the slice. So I guess that's why we ended up hiring him as our CFO and COO at Zappos.

We ended up doing the math a few years ago and figured out that, while I made more money from the pizza business than Alfred, he made about ten times more money *per hour* than me by arbitraging pizza. (There was also a lot less risk on his part. The grill was the victim of a burglary one night where $2,000 was stolen. At the end of the year, I figured I had effectively made about $2 an hour.)

I didn't know it at the time, but our pizza relationship was the seed that would lead to many million-dollar business opportunities together down the road.

As the end of my senior year in college approached, Sanjay introduced me to this thing called the World Wide Web. I thought it was a pretty interesting and fun thing to explore at the time, but I didn't pay too much attention to it.

The focus for most seniors, including myself, was trying to get a job lined up before graduation. A lot of companies from all over the country and from different industries sent recruiters to the Harvard campus so that we didn't need to travel to interview for our future jobs.

Many of our other roommates applied for banking or management consulting jobs, both of which were considered the "hot" jobs to get. To me, they both seemed incredibly boring, and I also heard that the workdays were sixteen hours long.

So Sanjay and I decided to interview mostly with technology companies. My goal was to find a high-paying job. I didn't really care what my specific job function was, what company I worked for, what the culture of the company was like, or where I ended up living.

I just wanted a job that paid well and didn't seem like too much work.

2

You Win Some, You Lose Some

Out in the Real World

Sanjay and I both got offers from Oracle.

I had a few different job offers, but it was a pretty easy decision to accept Oracle's. Not only did they offer me the most money ($40k per year in 1995 was pretty good pay for a job straight out of college), but they also were going to pay for moving all of the stuff I had accumulated during my college years to California, plus put Sanjay and me up in corporate housing for free for a few weeks while we were going through the training program for new hires.

I felt that I'd succeeded. I'd won the game of what I was told college was supposed to be all about: getting a job that paid as much money as possible. As I compared job offers that my other roommates had gotten, it was pretty clear that Sanjay and I were both going to be making more money than any of the rest of them.

A few months later, Sanjay and I were in the same new hire training class at Oracle together. This was a three-week program, and we were with twenty other people who had just graduated from college as well. Those three weeks flew by. It was basically a crash course in database programming. We had challenging and exciting projects. I really felt that I was learning a lot, making new friends, and most importantly, making good money. At the end of the training class, I was looking forward to meeting my new boss to start my new job.

I actually had no idea what I would be doing or what to expect. I really hadn't done any research on Oracle. All I knew was that they had sent someone to interview me on campus while I was in college and that they were impressed by my transcript. They really didn't know who I was, and I didn't really know who they were. I just knew I was supposed to be a "software engineer" and that they were paying me $40k.

On day 1 of my real job at Oracle, I was shown my desk and told what my ongoing tasks and responsibilities would be. Basically, I was supposed to be doing technical quality assurance and regression tests. I had no idea what that meant but it really didn't matter. I was making good money. And within a week, I learned that it was actually easy money too.

All I had to do was run a couple of tests every day. It took about five minutes to set up a test, and then about three hours for the automated test to run, during which time I would just be sitting around and waiting for the test to finish. So I could only run two or three tests a day at the most. I also realized that nobody was tracking what time I came in or left the office. In fact, I don't think anyone really even knew who I was.

For the first month or so, I felt incredibly lucky. I couldn't believe that I was getting paid good money to do something that took almost no effort. Sanjay and I had found an apartment that was seven minutes away from the office, and we were roommates once again.

Within a week, I had my daily routine down:

10:00 AM—Show up at my desk.

10:05 AM—Start running one of the tests.

10:10 AM—Check my e-mail, send e-mails to friends from my training class.

11:30 AM—Go home for lunch.

12:30 PM—Take a nap.
 1:45 PM—Head back to the office.
 2:00 PM—Start running another one of the tests.
 2:05 PM—Check my e-mail, respond to e-mails from friends in my training class.
 4:00 PM—Head back home.

I felt that I had lucked out because I had such an easy schedule, whereas Sanjay usually wouldn't get home until 7:00 PM. I would occasionally ask him how his job was, and he'd shrug and say something like "It's okay. Not that exciting."

I told him that my job was really not that exciting either, but maybe we could work on something during the evenings and weekends together for fun to help combat the boredom. There was that thing called the World Wide Web that was starting to become more and more popular. Sanjay was really good at graphic design, so maybe we could start something on the side where we could create Web sites for other companies.

The idea of starting our own side business sounded pretty fun. We decided to name the company Internet Marketing Solutions, or IMS for short. We created our own Web site, ordered a second phone line for our apartment, and went to Kinko's to print out some customized business cards. We were ready to start signing up some customers.

We had a plan for how to sign up customers: First, we would approach the local chamber of commerce and offer to build their Web site for free. Then we could tell all the local businesses that the chamber was a customer of ours (avoiding any mention that they were not paying us), sign up as many local businesses as possible, and the money would start rolling in soon after.

So, first things first. We had to get the chamber of commerce to let us build their Web site. Even though our pitch to them involved no money, approaching them was my first cold call over the phone, which led to my first in-person sales call. I had set up a meeting with them for 12:30 PM, which would fit in perfectly with my daily Oracle routine.

On the day of my appointment, I was nervous. I had never made a successful sales call before, but I knew my mission was to convince them that they needed a Web site and that we were the right partners for them. I knew that appearances were important, so when I left Oracle to go on my lunch break at 11:30 AM, I went home first and put on the suit and tie I had worn for graduation a few months earlier. I made sure that I had plenty of business cards. And I brought a few of our brochures that Sanjay had created and printed up a couple of days earlier.

Although I was nervous, the meeting went well. They were particularly receptive to the fact that we were offering to do everything for free. Over the next few weeks, my lunch breaks got longer and longer, and I ended up spending most of my time during the day meeting with the chamber to make sure they were happy with what we were creating for them. Sanjay's nights got longer and longer, as he was the one staying up all night actually creating their Web site. I was the sales and customer support guy, and he was the product and design guy. We made a good team.

We launched the chamber of commerce's Web site within a month, and now we were ready to start getting paying customers. Our first target was the Hillsdale mall, which was the big mall down the street from where we lived. We thought that would make a good choice because if we were able to sign them up as a customer, then we would be able to approach each of the stores inside and tell them that the mall itself had signed with us so they should as well.

Over the next couple of months, I spent less and less time in the office at Oracle as I met with the Hillsdale mall and other small businesses. We eventually convinced the mall to pay us $2,000 to design, manage, and host their entire Web site.

We had done it! We had our first real paying customer. We could quit our unfulfilling and boring day jobs at Oracle so we could run our own business full-time.

And so we decided that's what we were going to do.

I was a nervous wreck the morning that I was going to tell my boss at Oracle that I was quitting. After procrastinating for half an hour, I eventually worked up the courage to walk down the hallway to his office. I was ready to give him the news. Through his office window, he saw me approach and looked up. We made eye contact. I could feel my heart beating faster and faster. And then he looked away. I glanced over and realized at the last minute that he was meeting with someone else in his office, so I couldn't tell him right then. I felt a huge sense of relief, and continued walking past his office, pretending that I was actually just on my way to the bathroom down the hall.

So I washed my hands and waited inside the bathroom for another couple of minutes to make it seem like I actually had gone to the bathroom. And then I walked past my boss's office back to my desk and spent the next half hour e-mailing my friends. I figured that thirty minutes should be enough time for the meeting he was in to be over, but then I decided to wait another fifteen minutes after that just to be sure, and then started walking toward his office again.

For some reason, I was even more nervous the second time. I think maybe it's because I wasn't sure if he was still going to be meeting with whoever he was meeting with earlier. If he was still in that meeting, then I'd have to pretend I was making yet another trip to the bathroom, and he'd probably start thinking that I was maybe having some serious bladder or stomach issues. He was probably also thinking already that it was weird that I was using the bathroom close to his office instead of the one near my cubicle. But maybe he thought the one near me was out of order or something. I was pretty sure that all of these thoughts were running through his mind, so I was trying to convince myself that it didn't really matter, it was going to be my last day anyway. But in the back of my head, I kept thinking that all he would remember ten years later would be me needing to use the bathroom multiple times within a short period of time on the wrong side of the building. That would be disastrous.

So I resolved to make sure that his last memory of me was not "that weird guy who needed to go to the bathroom a lot." I had a plan. I would walk straight into his office and get this over with. So I marched over, telling myself that there was no turning back now. To make sure we didn't accidentally have any awkward eye contact beforehand, this time I walked closer to the wall so that he couldn't see me approach from far away. My heart racing, I saw that his door was open this time, and when I was finally in front of his door, I looked in, ready to tell him I was resigning.

Except there was nobody there.

This was going to go down in history as the most difficult resignation ever. I guess he had gone to another meeting or to lunch, so I decided to go to lunch as well. I would come back in the afternoon for Resignation Attempt Number Three.

So I let out a sigh and turned around. And ran right into my boss, who was behind me.

"Tony? Were you looking for me?" he asked.

I wasn't mentally prepared for this scenario. I'd been thinking about what value meal I was going to order from Taco Bell. Surprised and flustered, I hurriedly mumbled an awkward "no, sorry" and walked away as fast as I could without arousing any more suspicion.

At Taco Bell, I made two very important decisions. I decided to try their Double Decker Taco value meal, which turned out to have a surprisingly calming effect on my stomach. I also decided that I would wait until tomorrow to resign. Clearly I was being given signs that today was not the right day.

When I got back to the office later that afternoon, I was a lot more relaxed knowing that I didn't have to deal with resigning that day. I headed to the bathroom that was near my cubicle, only to be greeted with a sign on the door that said it was being cleaned and to please use the other bathroom—the one next to my boss's office.

Luckily for me, I was now quite familiar with the location of that bathroom, so I headed there. As I approached the bathroom, I saw that my boss was alone in his office with the door open. I impulsively decided I just wanted to get this over with, so before I could think too much about it, I forced myself to walk into his office.

"Do you have a few minutes?" I asked. I closed the door and sat down across from him. This was now the point of no return.

"I've…decided to resign," I said nervously. I'd only been at Oracle for five months and I hadn't really accomplished anything there. I didn't know how my boss would take the news. I was worried that he might be upset that I hadn't been at Oracle for very long and was already leaving. Or maybe he knew I had been taking long lunch breaks and was secretly happy that I was leaving. Or maybe he didn't care. The three seconds it took for him to respond seemed like three minutes.

"Wow! You must be joining another start-up! What an exciting opportunity!" He seemed genuinely excited and happy for me. He thought I was joining a company that had millions of dollars in venture-capital funding.

I didn't have the heart to tell him that I was just bored at Oracle and wanted to have time to make more sales calls for the Web design business that Sanjay and I were doing out of our living room. At the rate we were going, we would actually be making a lot less money than we were at Oracle.

But we wanted to run our own business and be in control of our own destiny. This wasn't about the money, it was about not being bored. Both Sanjay and I had now officially resigned, and we were ready to begin the next chapter of our lives. We had no idea where it would lead us, but wherever it was, we knew it had to be better than feeling bored and unfulfilled.

We were ready for an adventure.

Start-Up

As it turned out, the adventure we were waiting for to happen to us didn't end up happening on its own. We ended up sitting around in our apartment, occasionally doing some Web design work, and going out every once in a while to try to drum up some more sales.

By the end of the first week, it dawned on me that neither of us was actually passionate about doing Web design work. We loved the idea of owning and running our own business, but the reality ended up being a lot less fun than the fantasy.

My parents were not exactly thrilled that I'd quit my job at Oracle without a real plan for what to do next. When I told my dad that Sanjay and I were planning on running a Web design business, he told me that it didn't really sound like that could ever become a big-enough business to be meaningful. And now, one week into it, both Sanjay and I were starting to wonder if we'd made the right decision to leave Oracle.

The next few weeks were tough and somewhat depressing. We started to spend most of our time just surfing the Web to combat the boredom and to keep ourselves entertained. Watching Sanjay go into the coat closet to nap there in the middle of the day was only sort of funny the first time. We were starting to get a bit stir-crazy.

Luckily, we both had enough savings from the jobs we had in college that we didn't need to worry about whether we would be able to pay the rent for the rest of the year. We didn't know what we wanted to do, but we had learned what we *didn't* want to do. We didn't want to work for Oracle. We didn't want to do any more

Web design work. We didn't want to make any more sales calls. And we didn't want to be bored out of our minds.

So we spent our days and nights trying to figure out the next great Internet business idea, but we really couldn't come up with anything that sounded good. One weekend, out of sheer boredom, we decided to do some computer programming to test out an idea for something we initially called the Internet Link Exchange (ILE), which we eventually renamed to just LinkExchange.

The idea behind LinkExchange was pretty simple. If you ran a Web site, then you could sign up for our service for free. Upon signing up, you would insert some special code into your Web pages, which would cause banner ads to start showing up on your Web site automatically.

Every time a visitor came to your Web site and saw one of the banner ads, you would earn half a credit. So, if you had a thousand visitors come to your Web site every day, you would end up earning five hundred credits per day. With those five hundred credits, your Web site would be advertised five hundred times across the LinkExchange network for free, so this was a great way for Web sites that didn't have advertising budgets to gain additional exposure for free. The extra five hundred advertising impressions left over would be for us to keep. The idea was that we would grow the LinkExchange network over time and eventually have enough advertising inventory to hopefully sell to large corporations.

Sanjay and I finished all of the computer programming for our experiment over a weekend, and then we sent e-mails to fifty of our favorite small Web sites that we had found while surfing, asking them if they'd like to help test out our new service.

To our surprise, more than half the Web sites we e-mailed signed up to help us test out the service within twenty-four hours. As people visited their Web sites and saw the banner ads, word started to spread about LinkExchange. Within a week, we knew that our project that was initially meant to fight boredom had the potential to turn into something big. We decided that we should focus all of our energy on making LinkExchange a successful business.

The next five months were a bit of a whirlwind. Every day, more and more Web sites were signing up for our service. We weren't really worried about trying to make money yet. We were just focused on growing the size of the LinkExchange network. We were excited to be creating something that was growing quickly and that other people really seemed to appreciate using.

Sanjay and I were working around the clock, spending half our time doing computer programming and the other half answering customer service e-mails. We were religious about trying to answer every e-mail that came in as quickly as possible. Usually we were able to answer them within ten minutes, and people were amazed at our responsiveness.

We got to the point where we couldn't keep up with doing all the e-mail ourselves, so a friend who was visiting from out of town decided to help out and ended up never leaving. It was an exciting, fun, magical, and surreal time for all of us. We knew we were on to something big, we just had no idea how it would turn out. All the days started blurring together. We literally had no idea what day of the week it was.

One day in August 1996, we received a phone call from a guy named Lenny. He was calling from New York and he said he wanted to buy advertising on our network and also explore the possibility of us selling the company to him. Sanjay and I agreed to meet him later that week in San Francisco for dinner.

We met at Tony Roma's, a restaurant chain that specialized in all sorts of ribs. Lenny introduced himself as Bigfoot, which was apparently both the name of his company as well as his nickname. He ordered a Kahlúa drink, so I got the same thing. Sanjay, however, avoided the Kahlúa. He and Kahlúa had not been on good terms ever since that night that our college roommates forever refer to as "Kahlúa night," when a few too many Kahlúa drinks were consumed (and later vomited back out into the toilet that we all shared as roommates).

Lenny told us he wanted to make us an offer: $1 million in cash and stock for us to sell LinkExchange to Bigfoot. As part of the deal, Lenny wanted us to move to New York to work for Bigfoot. Sanjay and I looked at each other, both of us in shock. LinkExchange was only five months old, and we now had the opportunity to sell it for $1 million. This could be a life-changing opportunity for us. We told Lenny we wanted a few days to think about it, but the only word that I could think of in my head was *Wow*.

Sanjay and I spent the next twenty-four hours talking about what we should do. We really believed that LinkExchange had the potential to be so much bigger, but it was also hard to turn down so much money. So we decided to tell Lenny that we would sell the company for $2 million cash. This way, Sanjay and I would be able to walk away with $1 million each after only five months of work. I had read somewhere that you're in your best negotiating position if you don't care what the outcome is and you're not afraid to walk away. At $2 million, I would be happy whether the deal happened or not.

As it turned out, Lenny didn't think we were worth $2 million (and I don't think he actually had $2 million either), so we agreed to go our separate ways but continue to keep in touch.

"LinkExchange is a once-in-a-lifetime opportunity," Lenny said. "I've made a lot of money in my lifetime, but I've also lost a lot of money when I decided to bet the farm instead of taking money off the table. I wish you the best of luck."

Sanjay and I were more motivated than ever to make sure that LinkExchange would be successful. We had to prove Lenny wrong.

As more and more people signed up for our service, Sanjay and I realized that we needed a lot more help, both on the customer service side of things as well as with computer programming. In addition to convincing friends who were visiting us from out of town not to go home and instead help us answer e-mails, we also started looking for more computer programmers.

I remembered that in college, I had been in an international computer programming competition. Each college was allowed to send a team of their best three computer programmers to compete against teams from the other colleges. The team I was on ended up winning first place in the competition. I decided that I should reach out to Hadi, who had been one of my teammates during one of my years on the team, to see if he would be interested in joining LinkExchange.

Back in college, I'd learned that Hadi was interested in magic, so we had briefly discussed the idea of putting on a magic show in the college amphitheater as a way of possibly earning some extra cash. We thought we could be the next David Copperfield duo, but in the end it never went anywhere because we were both too busy.

When I contacted Hadi, I asked him if he'd be interested in joining LinkExchange, and I gave him all the background information about how quickly we were growing, the $1 million offer we had just turned down, and how exciting everything was. He told me that it definitely did sound exciting, but he was busy in Seattle working at Microsoft, heading up the team that would launch a Web browser called Internet Explorer to compete with the Netscape browser, so he wouldn't be able to join.

However, he told me he had a twin brother who looked just like him, and acted just like him. The two of them were so similar, he told me, that in college they used to go to each other's job interviews and pretend to be the other person if one of them was too busy. I wondered whether they ever pretended to be each other when going on blind dates.

"So ... you basically want us to hire your stunt double ... ?" I asked.

"Yeah."

"Is that story about you going on job interviews for each other true?"

"Yeah."

"Okay, sounds good. What's your stunt double's name?"

"Ali."

So after one meeting with Ali at our apartment, Sanjay and I decided to make him our third partner at LinkExchange, and we opened up a real office in San Francisco. Each of us started recruiting our friends to join LinkExchange, and one by one, they did.

By December of that year, there were twenty-five employees at LinkExchange, and most of them were friends of ours. That's when Jerry Yang, the co-founder of Yahoo!, said he wanted to meet with us. Yahoo! had just had a very high-profile and successful IPO earlier that year, and was worth over $1 billion. Jerry was the poster child for the dot-com craziness of the time, so we were all pretty excited to get to meet an Internet celebrity. We were hopeful that we'd be able to work out some sort of advertising deal with Yahoo! to help accelerate our growth.

As it turned out, Jerry wasn't interested in an advertising deal. He was interested in buying us, which came as a bit of a shock. We had to wait until the holidays were over because everyone in their corporate development office was on vacation, so we agreed to talk again in January.

After the New Year, he came and met with us in our old apartment and told Sanjay, Ali, and me the ballpark number of what they were willing to pay.

"Twenty million dollars."

I tried my hardest not to flinch and to appear as calm as possible. The first thought that came to my mind was *Wow*. The second thought that came to my mind was *I'm so glad we didn't sell the company to Lenny five months ago.*

We told Jerry that we would think about it and get back to him in a few days. This whole situation felt like déjà vu, except this time the numbers were bigger. Much, much bigger.

The next few days were filled with a lot of angst. We had told the rest of our employees what had happened, and that Sanjay, Ali, and I would be making the final decision. If we took the $20 million, I wouldn't have to work again for the rest of my life.

As a thought experiment, I made a list of all the things I would do with the money if I had it:

- I would buy a condo or loft in San Francisco so that I'd have a place to live that I could call my own, instead of renting a place and living with a roommate.
- I would buy a big-screen TV and build a home theater.
- I would want to be able to go on mini vacations (long weekends) whenever I wanted to, to places like Las Vegas, New York, Miami, and LA.
- I would buy a new computer.
- I would start another company, because I really enjoyed the idea of building and growing something.

I was surprised that my list was so short, and that it was actually pretty difficult for me to add anything else to it. With the savings I had from my previous jobs, I actually already had the ability to buy the TV and computer, and go on mini vacations. I just could never bring myself to do it.

I was already helping run a company that I was excited about. It seemed kind of silly to sell a company that I was excited about in order to start another company to be excited about. With the exception of actually owning my own place instead of renting, I realized that I already had the means to buy everything I wanted to buy.

Lenny's words rang through my head over and over again: "LinkExchange is a once-in-a-lifetime opportunity." I knew in my heart that, even if we failed, going after the opportunity was the right thing to do. It was much more important than owning a condo or loft at the age of twenty-three. Becoming a homeowner could wait until later in life.

I talked to Sanjay and Ali about my thought process, and they had independently come up with the same conclusion. We were still young. We could afford to be bold.

The next day we had a company meeting to announce our decision.

"As you all know, we received a term sheet from Yahoo! offering to buy the company, and we've been spending the last few days thinking about whether to accept their offer or not," I began. You could feel the tension building in the room.

"We've decided to turn down their offer."

As I looked around the room, I was surprised that there seemed to be a sense of relief in people's faces. "We are living in a very special time," I said. "The Internet industry is exploding. Companies like Netscape, eBay, Amazon, and Yahoo! are changing the course of human history. Never before have so many companies become successes in such a short period of time. We have the opportunity to be one of those companies while having the time of our lives."

I'm not sure why, but for some reason I started feeling more and more emotional. My voice started shaking. I had to get my final words out and end the meeting, or else I would start crying:

"There will never be another 1997."

It was us against the world, and we were going to make sure we would win.

The next few months were a blur. Somehow, everything seemed to fall into place as if there was someone watching over us making sure that we could do no wrong. Michael Moritz from Sequoia Capital, the same venture-capital firm that funded Yahoo!, became our board member and invested $3 million for a 20 percent stake in the company. More and more Web sites started signing up for our service, and we started signing some big advertisers to bring in revenue for the company. We hired a lot of smart, passionate employees (many of whom were friends of existing employees), and we had a lot of fun together. We were on top of the world.

I'm not quite sure how it started, but we had a really fun tradition at LinkExchange. Once a month, I'd send an e-mail out to the entire company letting them know that we were having an important meeting, and that some of our important investors and board members would be attending, so everyone was required to wear a suit and tie on the day of the meeting.

Everyone except for the most recently hired employees knew that it wasn't a real business meeting, and that they didn't actually need to wear a suit and tie. The real reason for the meeting was so that we could initiate and haze all the new employees who had joined LinkExchange in the past month.

So once a month, all the newly hired employees would show up to the office dressed up in suits and ties. There they would realize that they were the target of the companywide practical joke. In the afternoon meeting, all the new hires would be called up to the front of the room to complete some sort of embarrassing task.

After the Sequoia investment, we asked Michael Moritz to attend our initiation meeting, and we called him up to the front of the room along with the other six employees who had been hired in the past month.

After each person introduced himself, we let them know that in honor of Moritz's presence, we decided that we wanted everyone to move together in unison to the music that was about to be played.

If you've ever read anything in the media about Moritz, he's generally portrayed as an intelligent, introspective, and proper British journalist-turned-venture-capitalist, so everyone was excited to see that he was willing to stand in front of the room with the other new employees. Someone brought out a boom box and turned on the power as everyone started clapping and cheering. And then the music started playing. It was the *Macarena*.

I don't think words can ever truly describe what watching Moritz being forced to do the *Macarena* was like. It ranks up there as one of the strangest sights to behold. Everyone in the entire room was cheering and laughing, and by the end of the song I had tears streaming down my face from laughing so hard.

I remember looking around the room at all the happy faces and thinking to myself, *I can't believe this is real*. It wasn't just about Moritz doing the *Macarena* or that everyone in the entire room was laughing. It was about everything that had happened in the past year. It just didn't seem real.

In the words of *Pretty Woman*, I was living the fairy tale.

Rapid Growth

Shortly after we received funding from Sequoia, I reached out to Alfred, the guy I'd sold pizza to in college, to see if he would join us full-time. He was busy working on getting his PhD in statistics from Stanford. To me, that sounded like the second most boring thing to do in the world (the most boring being watching paint dry at night, when it's too dark to see what color the paint is).

Over the previous two years, I had been trying to figure out some sort of business we could do together. One of my earlier ideas was to open up a Subway sandwich franchise with Alfred somewhere on the Stanford campus. At the time, Subway was one of the fastest-growing franchises in the United States, partly because the franchise fee and start-up costs were so low. Alfred had actually considered doing it with me, but discovered that Stanford did not allow commercial activities on their campus at the time.

When Sanjay and I first started LinkExchange, I had asked Alfred whether he wanted to join. He thought it was too risky at the time and was also worried that his parents would get mad at him for dropping out of grad school, so we agreed to stay in touch and instead have him work as a consultant for us from time to time.

This time, however, Alfred was a lot more receptive. I think it was due to the combination of knowing that we had $3 million in the bank from Sequoia and him realizing that getting a PhD was not really his thing. He joined LinkExchange full-time in 1997 as our VP of finance.

Over the next seventeen months, all of us slept very little. We were growing very quickly and hiring people as fast as we could. We had pretty much exhausted our network of friends for hiring employees, so we started hiring almost any warm body who was willing to work for us and hadn't done more than six months of jail time.

We outgrew the floor we had rented out for our office and started expanding to additional floors of our building. We even opened up sales offices in New York and Chicago. It was a strange feeling to be walking around the office and seeing people I didn't recognize. It seemed like every week, there was someone new. It wasn't just that I didn't know people's names or what their jobs were... I didn't even recognize their faces. Walking up and down the stairs of our building, I wasn't sure if the people I ran into worked for LinkExchange or one of the other companies that shared our office building.

At the time, I didn't think it was necessarily a bad thing. If anything, not recognizing people due to our hypergrowth made things even more exciting and fueled the 24/7 adrenaline high that we were all feeling. But looking back, it should have been a huge warning sign for what was to come.

The short story is that we simply didn't know we should have paid more attention to our company culture. During the first year, we'd hired our friends and people who wanted to be part of building something fun and exciting. Without realizing it, we had together created a company culture that we all enjoyed being a part of.

Then, as we grew beyond twenty-five people, we made the mistake of hiring people who were joining the company for other reasons. The good news was that the people we hired were smart and motivated. The bad news was that many of them were motivated by the prospect of either making a lot of money or building their careers and résumés. They wanted to put a few years of hard work into LinkExchange and then move on to their next résumé-building job at another company. Or, if things worked out well, make a lot of money and retire. We continued to grow and hire more and more people, and eventually we had over a hundred employees in the company in 1998.

One day, I woke up after hitting the snooze button on my alarm clock six times. I was about to hit it a seventh time when I suddenly realized something. The last time I had snoozed this many times was when I was dreading going to work at Oracle. It was happening again, except this time, I was dreading going to work at LinkExchange.

This was a really weird realization for me. I was the co-founder of LinkExchange, and yet the company was no longer a place I wanted to be at. It wasn't always like this. Just a year and a half ago, I had made the "There will never be another 1997" speech to our employees. How did things change so quickly? What happened? How did we go from an "all-for-one, one-for-all" team environment to one that was now all about politics, positioning, and rumors?

Reflecting on the past year, I couldn't think of a single point in time when things started going downhill and it became less fun for me. There wasn't a specific employee I could point to who had single-handedly caused the company culture to deteriorate.

It was more like death by a thousand paper cuts, or like the Chinese water torture. Drop by drop, day by day, any single drop or bad hire was bearable and not that big a deal. But in the aggregate, it was torture.

I wasn't quite sure what to do. I pushed the thought out of my mind because there were some more immediate and urgent issues that we had to deal with: The economy wasn't doing well (something to do with Russian currency issues and Long Term Capital collapsing that I didn't quite understand), and the company didn't have much of a cash cushion to continue running if our revenues were to suddenly dry up. We had started doing the work for an IPO so that we could raise some more cash, but the Russian currency fiasco erased the possibility of that happening anytime soon. We needed to raise a "mezzanine" round of funding as insurance in case the economy got any worse. Otherwise, we could be bankrupt before the end of the year.

Over the previous two years, we had built pretty good relationships with people from Yahoo!, Netscape, and Microsoft. Each of those companies had shown a lot of interest in what we were doing and was interested in figuring out strategic partnership opportunities. (I never actually did figure out what a "strategic partnership" meant and how it was different from just a regular partnership, but everyone who said it sounded smarter so we liked to use that phrase a lot.)

To our surprise, all three of the companies said they were interested in possibly investing in our mezzanine round of financing. Even more surprising, Netscape and Microsoft both said that they were even more interested in buying the entire company outright.

We told them that the price tag was going to be at least $250 million. I'm not sure how we came up with that number, but it sounded good to me, and I guess it was a good sign that Netscape and Microsoft both said they wanted to continue talking.

They ended up getting into a bidding war.

In the end, Microsoft offered the biggest number—$265 million—but there were some strings attached to it. They wanted Sanjay, Ali, and me to stay with LinkExchange for at least another twelve months. If I stayed the entire time, then I would walk away with close to $40 million. If I didn't, then I would have to give up about 20 percent of that amount.

Even though LinkExchange was no longer fun for me, I

figured that I could stick around for another year at that rate. I just had to do the bare minimum amount of work so that I wouldn't get fired.

This practice of sticking around but not really doing anything was actually pretty common practice in Silicon Valley in acquisition scenarios. In fact, there's even a phrase that entrepreneurs use for this: "Vest In Peace."

The deal was signed a few weeks after our negotiations with Microsoft began. Compared with other acquisitions that Microsoft had done, the LinkExchange acquisition was done in record time, despite some behind-the-scenes drama internally.

Without getting into too much detail (and to protect the guilty), it was an education to me in human behavior and character. Large amounts of money have a strange way of getting people's true colors to come out. I observed the greed of certain people who had joined the company right before the acquisition trying to negotiate side contracts for themselves at the risk and expense of everyone else in the company. There was a lot of drama as people started fighting and trying to maximize the financial outcome only for themselves.

For myself personally, I decided to step away from the drama. It only confirmed in my mind that selling the company was the right thing to do, as I certainly did not want to be working with many of these people ever again. I just had to stick it through another twelve months.

One day in early November 1998, Sanjay and I went to lunch together at a restaurant a few blocks away from the LinkExchange office. The acquisition had already been covered by the press a couple of weeks earlier, but the deal had not yet officially closed. As we were finishing up our meal, Alfred called me on my cell phone and told me that it was now official. The deal had closed.

I looked at Sanjay and gave him the news. "Well, I guess the deal closed," I said. Both of us felt the same way. We weren't excited. We weren't cheering. We knew the outside world probably thought we were jumping up and down and doing cartwheels, but instead our mood was a strange mix of apathy and relief. The excitement of LinkExchange had disappeared long ago. Now we just had the drudgery of sticking around uninspired and unmotivated for another twelve months.

"I guess we should probably walk back to the office then," I said.

"Okay."

And so we did, in silence.

Cruise Control

A bet is a bet. If I lose a bet, I always pay up.

On graduation day in college, my friends made a bet with me. They bet that I would become a millionaire within ten years, and if it happened, then we would all go on a cruise together, and I would pay for everyone's trip. If it didn't happen, then we would still go on a cruise together, but they would pool together and pay for my trip. To me, it seemed like a win–win situation: either I would be a millionaire or I would get a free cruise. Either way, I would be happy, so I agreed to the bet.

It was early 1999, and we all flew to Florida to take a three-day cruise to the Bahamas. I decided to invite some of my other friends as well, so we ended up with a group of about fifteen people. I had never been on a cruise before, so I was pretty amazed at how big the ship was. There was a nightclub, ten bars, swimming pools, and five all-you-can-eat restaurants. We had a great time drinking, eating, partying, and then drinking, eating, and partying some more. It was like a mini college reunion, without all the boring parts.

We all decided to go to the nightclub on the final night of the cruise to drink and dance the night away. In the eyes of all of my friends on the cruise, I was everything that they thought defined success and happiness. My friends commented that I seemed more self-confident and congratulated me on selling the company to Microsoft.

At 1:00 AM, the DJ announced that it was last call, and that the bar and club would be shutting down soon. As everyone headed to the bar to get one last drink before the night was over, I stood by myself for a moment to avoid the rush and to take in the moment. If someone had told me four years ago that I would be a millionaire and on a cruise ship celebrating, I would not have believed it.

Yet, as the drinks flowed, the music pulsated, and friends cheered and toasted one another, a nagging voice in the back of my mind repeatedly brought up the same questions that had been there ever since the silent walk with Sanjay back to the office the day the Microsoft deal closed: *Now what? What's next?*

And then there were the follow-up questions: *What is success? What is happiness? What am I working toward?*

I still didn't have the answers. So I went to the bar, ordered a shot of vodka, and clinked glasses with Sanjay. Figuring out the answers could wait until later.

After the cruise, I felt like I was on autopilot: waking up late, making an appearance at the office for a few hours and checking my e-mail, then heading home early. Every once in a while, I'd skip going to the office altogether.

I had a lot of free time and I didn't know what to do with it.

So I had a lot of time to think. I'd already bought all the things I wanted: a place to live, a big-screen TV, a computer, and a home theater system. I started going to Vegas every other weekend to play poker. I wasn't playing for the money. It was about the challenge of figuring out how to beat the game. Poker is the only casino game where you're playing against other players instead of the house, so as long as you're better than the average player at your table, you actually can win in the long run.

But most of my free time was spent just being introspective

and thinking. I didn't need more money, so what was it good for? I wasn't spending the money I already had. So why was I staying at Microsoft, vesting in peace, trying to get more of it?

I made a list of the happiest periods in my life, and I realized that none of them involved money. I realized that building stuff and being creative and inventive made me happy. Connecting with a friend and talking through the entire night until the sun rose made me happy. Trick-or-treating in middle school with a group of my closest friends made me happy. Eating a baked potato after a swim meet made me happy. Pickles made me happy. (Although for that one, I'm still unclear why. I think it's just because they are obviously delicious and I enjoy saying "pickles.")

I thought about how easily we are all brainwashed by our society and culture to stop thinking and just assume by default that more money equals more success and more happiness, when ultimately happiness is really just about enjoying life.

I thought about how I enjoyed creating, building, and doing stuff that I was passionate about. And there was so much opportunity to create and build stuff, especially with the Internet still exploding, and not enough time to pursue every idea out there. And yet here I was, wasting my time, wasting my life, so that I could make more money even though I had all the money I ever needed for the rest of my life. A lot was going to change about the world. We were on the eve of not only a new century, but a new millennium. The world was about to change in a dramatic way, and I was about to miss out on it so that I could make even more money when I already had all the money I would ever need.

And then I stopped thinking to myself and started talking to myself:

"There will never be another 1999. What are you going to do about it?"

I already knew the answer. In that moment, I had chosen to be true to myself and walk away from the all the money that was keeping me at Microsoft.

A few days later, I went to the office, sent my good-bye e-mail to the company, and walked out the door. I didn't know exactly what I was going to do, but I knew what I wasn't going to do. I wasn't going to sit around letting my life and the world pass me by. People thought I was crazy for giving up all that money. And yes, making that decision was scary, but in a good way.

I didn't realize it at the time, but it was a turning point for me in my life. I had decided to stop chasing the money, and start chasing the passion.

I was ready for the next chapter in my life.

3

Diversify

New Ventures

"Now what?"

Many of us left LinkExchange at around the same time, and we were all trying to answer the same question. We'd just made a lot of money from the sale of the company to Microsoft, and we were supposed to be basking in the fruits of our labor.

But many of us didn't have any great answers.

I thought back to my childhood fantasies. I'd wanted to work for the CIA in a James Bond type of role, become a robot inventor, and find a place to live with a movie theater and Taco Bell downstairs.

I no longer wanted to be a spy or a robot inventor, but living above a movie theater still appealed to me. As luck would have it, I happened to be driving around one day and saw that AMC was opening up a big new movie theater complex right in the heart of San Francisco at 1000 Van Ness. There would be fourteen different theaters, and right above the lobby of the theaters, fifty-three brand-new lofts were about to go on sale. When I learned that there was a Taco Bell less than two blocks away, I knew it was a sign. This was going to be my future home.

I learned that real estate developers had actually taken over an entire city block and combined two buildings to create this space. In addition to the lofts and movie theaters, there was also a gym, an area designated for a future restaurant, and some commercial space that hadn't yet been leased out.

I told other ex-LinkExchangers about the space. I thought back to my college years, when there was a core group of us who always hung out together. We could create our own adult version of a college dorm and build our own community. It was an opportunity for us to create our own world. It was perfect.

One by one, our crew started moving into the lofts. Alfred ended up living two doors down from me. By the time all of us had moved in, we collectively owned 20 percent of the lofts in that building and controlled 40 percent of the board seats of the home-owners' association. It was like we were playing our own private real-life version of Monopoly. And nothing could compare to the spontaneity and convenience of being able to stroll over in pajamas to a friend's place or to the movie theater.

While we were in the process of moving in to our new homes, Alfred and I decided to start an investment fund. A friend of ours had a pet frog in college, and she dared us to name the fund and incubator Venture Frogs.

So of course we did.

We ended up raising $27 million from ex-LinkExchange employees, and started meeting with a lot of different companies. We decided to turn one of the one-bedroom lofts into our office and set up a couple of computers and phones there.

One day, I received a voice mail from a guy named Nick Swinmurn, who said he had just started a Web site called shoesite.com. His idea was to build the Amazon of shoes and create the world's largest shoe store online.

To me, it sounded like the poster child of bad Internet ideas. Other companies were selling pet food and furniture online and losing large sums of money in the process. In my mind, it seemed like there was no way people would be willing to buy shoes online without trying them on first.

I reached over to the phone and just as I was about to delete the voice mail, Nick threw out a few statistics: Footwear was a $40 billion industry in the United States, and 5 percent of that was already being done by paper mail-order catalogs. It was also the fastest-growing segment of the industry.

I did some quick math and realized that 5 percent was equal to $2 billion. It didn't matter whether I would be willing to buy shoes without trying them on first. What mattered was that consumers were already doing it, and it seemed pretty reasonable to assume that Web sales would one day be at least as big as catalog sales. Alfred and I decided it was at least worth a meeting.

We had an informal meeting with Nick in our loft. He was dressed casually, wearing board shorts and a T-shirt. He looked like he could have still been in college, just stopping by to chat with us during his lunch break.

We didn't pretend we had a real office, and Nick didn't pretend he had much more than an idea, but it was clear that he was passionate about the opportunity. Nick told us he had just graduated from college a few years earlier.

Nick summarized his entire pitch in three sentences: "Footwear is a $40 billion industry in the United States, of which catalog sales make up $2 billion. It is likely that e-commerce will continue to grow. And it is likely that people will continue to wear shoes in the foreseeable future."

"Do you have any experience in the footwear industry?" Alfred asked.

"No, but I walked around a shoe show in Las Vegas a few months ago and some of the people said they thought it was an interesting idea."

"Maybe you should find someone with footwear experience," I said.

"Yeah. That sounds like a good idea," Nick replied.

We decided to stay in touch and agreed to set up another meeting once Nick had found someone to join the company who had experience in the footwear industry. I also suggested that Nick come up with another name. Calling the Web site "Shoesite" seemed too generic, and it limited the business from eventually expanding into other product categories.

How I Got the Original Idea
by Nick

Buying a pair of shoes shouldn't be so hard, I remember thinking. Store after store, mall after mall, I couldn't find a single pair. It wasn't as if I was living in Smalltown, USA, either. If I couldn't find shoes worth buying in the Bay Area, I could only imagine the kind of trouble people had elsewhere.

At the time, there were just a bunch of mom-and-pop stores on the Web that didn't make shoe shopping any easier. So I thought, why not create a single place online that people could come to, find exactly the shoe they want in exactly the right size, and have it show up on their doorstep in a few days? It was such a simple idea, why wasn't anyone doing it?

It was brilliant until I discovered the reason—it wasn't going to be easy. The shoe industry was extremely fragmented and not very tech-savvy. But if I could figure out a way to create a network among all the separate shoe stores, that could be the solution.

I went ahead and reserved the domain name Shoesite. com. With the site ready to go, I just needed one other thing—shoes.

I headed down to the local shoe store, took pictures of their stock, and put them on the Web site. Every time someone bought something on the site, I'd buy it from the store and ship it to them.

For a big believer in technology, I couldn't have found a more primitive way to do it.

But it worked. People started buying shoes. I didn't have the faintest clue about the workings of the shoe industry, but I knew I was on to something. Even though I'd never bought a pair of shoes through mail order, statistics proved there were a ton of people doing it. I stopped thinking, *Hey, this is a good idea,* and started believing in it. Somehow, I had to make it work.

A few weeks later, Nick contacted us and said that he wanted to set up a lunch meeting. He'd found someone named Fred who worked in the men's shoe department at Nordstrom and was interested in joining the company, but only if the company got funding beyond the small friends-and-family round that Nick had already raised. Nick also asked me what I thought of "Zapos" as the name for the company, derived from *zapatos,* which was the Spanish word for "shoes." I told him that he should add another *p* to it so that people wouldn't mispronounce it and accidentally say *ZAY-pos.*

And thus, the name Zappos was born.

A few days later, Alfred and I met with Nick and Fred at Mel's, a 1950s-themed diner a block away from where we lived. As we talked about the potential of Zappos, I did my best to not let the fact that Fred was a spitting image of Nicolas Cage distract me from the business conversation. Fred was thirty-three years old, tall, and really did look like he could be Nicolas Cage's stunt double.

I ordered the turkey melt, with a side of chicken noodle soup to dip the sandwich in. Fred ordered a turkey burger. Exactly ten years later, Fred and I would return to Mel's and order the same thing to celebrate our ten-year meeting-versary together.

Nick talked about the progress that the Web site had made over the past few weeks. They were already getting $2,000 worth of orders a week, and the numbers were growing. They weren't making any money, because anytime an order was placed, Nick would run to the local shoe store, buy the item, and then ship it out to the customer. Nick wanted to put up the Web site just to prove that people would actually be willing to buy shoes online.

There were literally thousands of different brands in the footwear industry. The real business idea was to eventually form partnerships with hundreds of brands, and have each of the brands provide Zappos with an inventory feed of what was in each of their warehouses. Zappos would take orders from customers on the Internet, then transmit the order to the manufacturer of each brand, which would then ship directly to the Zappos customer.

This was known as a "drop ship" relationship, and although it already existed in many other industries, drop shipping had never been done before in the footwear industry. Nick and Fred were betting that they would be able to convince the brands at the next shoe show to start drop shipping, and then Zappos would not have to own any inventory or worry about running a warehouse.

Fred told us that he'd climbed the corporate ladder at Nordstrom for eight years, just bought a house, and just had his first kid. He knew that joining Zappos would be a big risk, but he was ready to take a leap of faith if Venture Frogs would provide the seed funding for the company.

Alfred and I looked at each other. Nick and Fred were exactly the type of people we were looking to invest in. We didn't know if the shoe idea would work or not, but they were clearly passionate and willing to place big bets.

We decided that we would invest enough money so that Zappos could hire more employees and meet payroll through the end of the year. The idea was that if the company was progressing and doing well by the end of the year, then Zappos could raise a lot more money from a venture-capital firm such as Sequoia. We felt confident that since Sequoia had made out with more than $50 million from their $3 million investment in LinkExchange, they would be willing to place another bet on a company that Alfred and I were involved in.

A week after our seed investment, Fred quit his job at Nordstrom. He was officially a Zappos employee now. He and Nick headed to the shoe show in Las Vegas the very next day.

My First Shoe Show as a Zappos Employee
by Fred

I went to Las Vegas for the WSA (World Shoe Association) shoe show the next day as a Zappos employee. I'm not quite sure what we were thinking, but we showed up without a Power-Point presentation or any marketing collateral. We just had a sheet of paper and an idea.

We talked to eighty different brands over the next four days. Only three agreed to work with us. It wasn't exactly a promising number, but it wasn't surprising either. We were pioneering a new concept of having brands drop ship directly from their inventory to the customer.

Talking to the brands was actually educational because they asked legitimate questions like, "How are you going to ship it? Who's your shipping carrier? How do you plan to handle returns?"

At least we now knew a lot of things about what we didn't know. We retreated to our hotel room for lunch and asked ourselves what we needed to do.

So we started cold-calling. We left messages with DHL, UPS, and FedEx. After some nail-biting and a lot of idea-throwing, we finally got a reply. UPS was the only one that called us back and it turned out it was the only one we needed. They believed in us from the beginning and they're still great partners with us now.

> Looking back, a lot of our growth happened that way. We'd
> just throw ideas against the wall to see if they'd stick, improvise,
> and make it happen.

Alfred and I weren't very involved with Zappos during the
first few months after we made the investment. We were busy
meeting with other companies that were looking for seed investments. Over the course of the next year, we would make twenty-
seven different investments, and we would check in with each of
the different companies, including Zappos, about once every two
weeks to see how they were progressing.

To me, it was a bit of a strange shift to not be involved in the
day-to-day details of the companies that we were now investors in.
Once the investment had been made, we would occasionally offer
advice to anyone who asked for it, but for the most part the companies were busy running on their own.

I was getting bored with the investment business, so I started
looking for something else to fill my time. I wanted to find something that was both fun and challenging at the same time.

That's when I discovered poker.

Poker

I'd played a little bit of poker in college, but like many people, I
always just considered it to be a fun form of gambling and had
never bothered to actually study it. Back in 1999, poker was not yet
a mainstream activity. Most people had never heard of the World
Series of Poker, and TV networks like ESPN were not yet broad-
casting poker tournaments to the masses.

One night while battling insomnia, I randomly came across
a Web site that served as a community hub for people who played
poker regularly. I was fascinated by the amount of analysis and
information about playing that was freely available, and spent the

entire night reading different articles about the mathematics of poker.

Like many people, I had always thought that poker was mostly about luck, being able to bluff, and reading people. I learned that for limit hold 'em poker (which was the most popular type of poker in casinos at the time), none of that really mattered much in the long run. For every hand and every round of betting, there was actually a mathematically correct way to play that took into account the "pot odds" (the ratios among the amount of the bet, the number of chips already in the pot, and the statistical chances of winning).

With the exception of poker, almost all games in a typical casino are stacked against the player, and in the long run the casino always comes out ahead. I was intrigued by poker because in poker you are playing against other players, not against the casino. Instead, the casino just takes a service fee for each hand dealt (usually from the winner of each hand).

In a casino, each poker table seats up to ten players. As long as at least one of the players is not playing in the mathematically optimal way (and usually it's several players that aren't), the players who are playing correctly will generally end up winning at the end of the day.

Learning the basic math behind limit hold 'em poker was not actually that hard. I bought and studied a book called *Hold 'em Poker* and started going to card rooms in California several times a week to practice what I was learning from the book. (Although California is a generally no-gambling state, card rooms are allowed because poker is not a game against the house.) Within a few weeks, I felt that I had mastered the basics of the mathematics behind playing hold 'em.

Understanding the mathematics behind hold 'em and playing against players who didn't was like owning a coin that would land on heads one-third of the time and tails the other two-thirds of the time, and always being allowed to bet on tails. On any individual coin flip, I might lose, but if I bet on tails a thousand times, then I was more than 99.99 percent guaranteed to win in the long run.

Likewise, when playing a game against the house such as roulette or blackjack, it would be like being forced to always bet on heads: Even though you might win any individual coin flip, if you did it a thousand times, you would be more than 99.99 percent guaranteed to lose in the long run.

One of the most interesting things about playing poker was learning the discipline of not confusing *the right decision* with *the individual outcome* of any single hand, but that's what a lot of poker players do. If they win a hand, they assume they made the right bet, and if they lose a hand, they often assume they made the wrong bet. With the coin that lands on heads a third of the time, this would be like seeing the coin land on heads once (*the individual outcome*) and changing your behavior so you bet on heads, when the mathematically correct thing to do is to always bet on tails no matter what happened in the previous coin flip (*the right decision*).

For the first few months, I found poker both fun and challenging, because I was constantly learning, both through reading different books and through the actual experience of playing in the field. I started to notice similarities between what was good poker strategy and what made for good business strategy, especially when thinking about the separation between short-term thinking (such as focusing on whether I won or lost an individual hand) and long-term thinking (such as making sure I had the right decision strategy).

I noticed so many similarities between poker and business that I started making a list of the lessons I learned from playing poker that could also be applied to business:

Evaluating Market Opportunities

- Table selection is the most important decision you can make.

- It's okay to switch tables if you discover it's too hard to win at your table.
- If there are too many competitors (some irrational or inexperienced), even if you're the best it's a lot harder to win.

Marketing and Branding

- Act weak when strong, act strong when weak. Know when to bluff.
- Your "brand" is important.
- Help shape the stories that people are telling about you.

Financials

- Always be prepared for the worst possible scenario.
- The guy who wins the most hands is not the guy who makes the most money in the long run.
- The guy who never loses a hand is not the guy who makes the most money in the long run.
- Go for positive expected value, not what's least risky.
- Make sure your bankroll is large enough for the game you're playing and the risks you're taking.
- Play only with what you can afford to lose.
- Remember that it's a long-term game. You will win or lose individual hands or sessions, but it's what happens in the long term that matters.

Strategy

- Don't play games that you don't understand, even if you see lots of other people making money from them.
- Figure out the game when the stakes aren't high.
- Don't cheat. Cheaters never win in the long run.
- Stick to your principles.

- You need to adjust your style of play throughout the night as the dynamics of the game change. Be flexible.
- Be patient and think long-term.
- The players with the most stamina and focus usually win.
- Differentiate yourself. Do the opposite of what the rest of the table is doing.
- Hope is not a good plan.
- Don't let yourself go "on tilt." It's much more cost-effective to take a break, walk around, or leave the game for the night.

Continual Learning

- Educate yourself. Read books and learn from others who have done it before.
- Learn by doing. Theory is nice, but nothing replaces actual experience.
- Learn by surrounding yourself with talented players.
- Just because you win a hand doesn't mean you're good and you don't have more learning to do. You might have just gotten lucky.
- Don't be afraid to ask for advice.

Culture

- You've gotta love the game. To become really good, you need to live it and sleep it.
- Don't be cocky. Don't be flashy. There's always someone better than you.
- Be nice and make friends. It's a small community.
- Share what you've learned with others.
- Look for opportunities beyond just the game you sat down to play. You never know who you're going to meet, including new friends for life or new business contacts.

- Have fun. The game is a lot more enjoyable when you're trying to do more than just make money.

Aside from remembering to focus on what's best for the long term, I think the biggest business lesson I learned from poker concerned the most important decision you can make in the game. Although it seems obvious in retrospect, it took me six months before I finally figured it out.

Through reading poker books and practicing by playing, I spent a lot of time learning about the best strategy to play once I was actually sitting down at a table. My big *"ah-ha!"* moment came when I finally learned that the game started even before I sat down in a seat.

In a poker room at a casino, there are usually many different choices of tables. Each table has different stakes, different players, and different dynamics that change as the players come and go, and as players get excited, upset, or tired.

I learned that the most important decision I could make was which table to sit at. This included knowing when to change tables. I learned from a book that an experienced player can make ten times as much money sitting at a table with nine mediocre players who are tired and have a lot of chips compared with sitting at a table with nine really good players who are focused and don't have that many chips in front of them.

In business, one of the most important decisions for an entrepreneur or a CEO to make is what business to be in. It doesn't matter how flawlessly a business is executed if it's the wrong business or if it's in too small a market.

Imagine if you were the most efficient manufacturer of seven-fingered gloves. You offer the best selection, the best service, and the best prices for seven-fingered gloves—but if there isn't a big enough market for what you sell, you won't get very far.

Or, if you decide to start a business that competes directly against really experienced competitors such as Wal-Mart by playing the same game they play (for example, trying to sell the same goods at lower prices), then chances are that you will go out of business.

In a poker room, I could only choose which table I wanted to sit at. But in business, I realized that I didn't have to sit at an existing table. I could define my own, or make the one that I was already at even bigger. (Or, just like in a poker room, I could always choose to change tables.)

I realized that, whatever the vision was for any business, there was always a bigger vision that could make the table bigger. When Southwest Airlines first started, they didn't see their target market as limited to just existing airline travelers, which was what all the other airlines did. Instead, they imagined their service as something that could potentially serve all the people who traveled by Greyhound bus or by train, and they designed their business around that. They offered short flights at cheap prices, instead of going with the more prevalent "hub and spoke" model that other airlines were using. They made it easy for customers to change flights without paying huge penalties. And they turned their planes around at airports as fast as possible. They succeeded because they decided to play at a different table than the one that all the other airlines were playing at.

Over a period of several months, I learned a lot about poker, but toward the end I started getting bored with playing in the California card rooms. Part of the reason was that I started noticing it was the same players who were showing up all the time, and many of them seemed to be playing full-time either because they didn't have anything else to do or were trying to win their rent money for the month. After I'd spent several months learning and practicing the mathematics of the game, playing limit hold 'em started to feel more and more mechanical, and less and less challenging.

So I started making weekend trips to Las Vegas, and found the game much more interesting there. I got to meet a lot of interesting people from all different backgrounds. Most of them didn't even live in Vegas, and many of them were running their own successful businesses as their full-time occupation. Poker was just a fun hobby that they occasionally did on the side.

I stopped playing in the California card rooms altogether. While I would continue to play poker throughout my life, poker stopped being a focus for me. I was far from a world-class player, but I had learned enough about the game that I was ready for something different. For me, the goal of all future poker games would no longer be trying to make money or improving my poker skills and experience. Moving forward, the goal and purpose of playing poker would be more about hanging out with friends, meeting interesting people, and building relationships.

I'd realized that whether in poker, in business, or in life, it was easy to get caught up and engrossed in what I was currently doing, and that made it easy to forget that I always had the option to change tables. Psychologically, it's hard because of all the inertia to overcome. Without conscious and deliberate effort, inertia always wins.

I'd started to force myself to think again about what I was trying to get out of life. I asked myself what I was trying to accomplish, what I wanted to do, and whether I should be sitting at a different table. From my poker experience, I knew it was never too late to change tables.

I realized that once I had learned the basics of poker, I wasn't really building anything by spending endless hours in casinos playing the game. I realized that I needed to be doing something more fulfilling, and that maybe I was no longer playing the right game. After what felt like an intensive summer fling with the game of poker, I decided it was time for me to move on to something new.

It was time for me to change tables.

Dabbling

As I tried to figure out what I wanted to do next, I ended up doing a whole lot of dabbling. I dabbled in "investing" and day-trading, putting money into the stock market in companies that I knew nothing about, and ended up losing a lot of money. I decided to invest in a movie called *Christmas in the Clouds,* in which I had a small cameo role. I ended up losing a lot of money in that too.

They were expensive lessons, but I guess what I ended up learning was that it's a bad idea to invest in industries you don't understand, in companies you don't have any control or influence over, or in people you don't know or trust.

Over time, I also kept asking myself why I was investing in anything at all. What was my goal? To make more money? That didn't make sense, since I had already given up a lot of money when I walked away from Microsoft.

I realized that the day-trading and investing I was doing weren't really fulfilling. I didn't feel like I was really building anything. It felt more like I was gambling, but with the odds stacked against me because I was investing money in things I didn't understand. I ultimately made the decision to pull out of almost all my stock market investments and to try to figure out something more meaningful to focus on instead.

I had been checking in every week or two with the folks at Zappos, offering advice (especially on the technology side) as needed. It was just a handful of people working at Zappos, but they were making good progress for such a small team.

Alfred and I introduced Zappos to Michael Moritz at Sequoia and helped set up an initial meeting. We felt good. The Zappos team was passionate about what they were doing, they were making great progress, and Alfred and I had talked up Zappos to Sequoia in our e-mail introductions to them. We assured the Zappos folks that the meeting was more of a formality than a pitch. With their LinkExchange investment, Sequoia had turned a $3 million investment into over $50 million—basically multiplying their money by seventeen in just seventeen months. Alfred and I had credibility, and in our minds, it seemed like a relatively small thing to ask Sequoia for a few million dollars to put into Zappos.

What Happened Next
by Fred

It wasn't pleasant. It was December 10 and we knew we had until the fifteenth to raise more money. All we had was five days to find funding or Zappos would be out of business.

I was in New York, attending every single shoe show to sell Zappos as a company and sign on more footwear brands. We were doing all that we could, basically hustling, expecting that phone call from Nick to see if Zappos was going to survive.

I was having dinner at a restaurant when he broke the news. Sequoia decided not to invest. I had stepped outside to receive the call and when I sat back down at the table, the waiter accidentally spilled a glass of water in my lap. I had to laugh. When it rained, it literally poured.

After returning to California, Nick and I tried calling more venture capitalists to raise more money, but no one was willing to invest. On the afternoon of the fifteenth, all twelve of us in the company got together and did what most would naturally do—head down to Chevy's for a margarita.

We knew we had given it our best shot and recognized it was a good run. For us, it just didn't happen to work out. After a few rounds, we headed back to the office around four o'clock and started cleaning out our desks.

Alfred and I were both a bit surprised when we learned that Sequoia wasn't interested in investing in Zappos. We reached out to Sequoia to find out what had happened or if anything had gone wrong. We were told that the accomplishments of the team were impressive given how small the team was and that the company had only been around for a few months, but Sequoia wasn't confident that this would ever end up being more than a niche business. They wanted to see more growth and progress in the company, and they suggested that we touch base again in a few months.

Our original plan with Venture Frogs was to make a single small angel investment in each company and then pass them on to the bigger venture capital companies like Sequoia a few months afterward, so we were in a bit of a quandary with Zappos. Either we had to make another investment in Zappos with money from the Venture Frogs fund, or we had to let Zappos go out of business.

Letting Zappos go out of business would have fit in better with our original investment strategy and philosophy: Invest in a lot of different Internet companies with the expectation that a third would make money, a third would break even, and a third would go out of business. Zappos would simply fall into that last category.

"What do you want to do about Zappos?" Alfred asked. "We have to make a decision today. They only have a couple of days of cash left, and Sequoia isn't interested in putting money in them for at least a few months. They want to see more progress."

"If that happens, then they'll definitely fund them?" I asked.

"Not definitely," Alfred replied. "But I think more likely than not. It's definitely a risk. We can give Zappos a few months more of cash to tide them over to their next meeting with Sequoia and hope that Sequoia will invest at that time. But if Sequoia doesn't, then we're going to wind up in the same situation we're in right now, except there probably won't be much money left in our fund by then."

This was a tough call. If we decided to invest more money into Zappos, then that meant that we wouldn't be able to make an investment into another company.

"It's definitely higher risk. Sort of like putting more eggs into a basket," I said. "But I like the guys there. They're passionate and determined, and they don't seem like they're doing this just to get rich quick. They're actually interested in trying to build something for the long term."

"Well, if you think we should put more money into Zappos, then we really should be spending more time with them in order to protect our investment," Alfred said. "We should get them to move into the incubator."

As part of the investment strategy for our fund, Alfred and I had decided to start the Venture Frogs Incubator, where we would provide office space and services for Internet companies. It would also allow us to work more closely with whichever companies were in the incubator.

We had talked to the landlord of the building we lived in because there was still a lot of commercial space available for lease. Alfred and I decided to take over all of the remaining space. Our plan was to convert part of it into office space for the incubator and part of it into a restaurant. This way, there would be no reason for us and the companies we would incubate to leave the building. We would all be able to work longer and harder.

The problem was that the incubator space was still under construction.

"Yeah, I think that's a good idea, but the incubator isn't going to be ready for at least a few months," I said. "The next few months are going to be critical. They're going to make or break the company."

"So what do you want to do?" Alfred asked.

I thought about all the possible options.

"I have my birthday party this weekend, and a New Year's party in two weeks. Let's have them move into my loft right after New Year's. We'll convert it into an office until the incubator offices are ready downstairs."

"Sounds good."

The Phone Call
by Fred

As we were packing up our things that afternoon, we got a call that we didn't expect. It was Tony. He had decided to invest another three to four months' worth with a couple of conditions:

"You have to move into my loft in San Francisco, and I'm going to be much more involved in the company."

Up until that time, we had just been sending Tony a sales report once a week, and had seen him visit the office once with Alfred. We were busy running around, doing our thing. But with his call, it was obvious he could see Zappos' potential.

It was an easy decision to make.

We packed up and moved from Emeryville into his loft, and for the next twelve months, Tony would invest four months at a time. Imagine never knowing if you were going to have a job at the end of four months. It would come down to the very last day, when he'd decide whether he thought it was worthwhile. Fortunately for us, he did. So we just kept plugging away to make progress for those four-month cycles, wait to see if we've been given another four months of oxygen, and get right back to digging in to make things happen.

For that entire year, that's all we did. We hustled.

My Red Bull Relationship
by Tony

I have friends from all different walks of life. Some friends I enjoy hanging out with at bars. Some friends I enjoy watching movies with. Some friends I enjoy working with. Some friends I enjoy hiking with. And some friends I enjoy writing with, occasionally discussing what preposition not to end a sentence with.

One of the longest relationships I've been able to maintain in my life has been with Red Bull. We recently celebrated our ten-year anniversary together. We had originally met at a night-club in downtown San Francisco (a mutual friend introduced us), and had a great time dancing the night away. Over time, our activities together expanded beyond the nightclub scene and became more and more varied. I think the reason why Red Bull has become such an integral part of my life is because of its versatility and ability to adapt to almost any situation.

Red Bull has been my faithful companion almost every-where I go, no matter what activity I'm doing, including drinking at bars, watching movies, working in the office, and hiking in the mountains. In fact, I'm sipping a Red Bull as I'm writing this and sitting next to my writing friends who are having trouble comprehending why I would feel compelled to write about my relationship with Red Bull.

I guess at the end of the day, my thought is that it's pretty hard to find a good companion that's compatible with so many parts of your life and is always there to support you along the way. If you're able to find a companion that you wouldn't mind accompanying you to breakfast and to dinner, that helps you get through your post-lunch food coma at the office as well as your final miles in a marathon, and that you can enjoy with or without alcohol—that's a pretty rare thing to come across.

To me, that's a relationship worth keeping.

Connectedness

My birthday party was coming up, and I wanted to make sure that it was unlike any birthday party I had ever thrown before. I had decided to go all-out for it.

A few months earlier, I'd reconnected with some friends from high school, and similar to my college days, a core group of about fifteen of us formed and we started hanging out with each other several times a week. In the beginning, it wasn't purposeful or planned. It was just a by-product of the fact that there were already so many of us living in the same building, so impromptu gatherings became more and more common.

Sometimes we would hang out in someone's loft, and other times we would all plan on going to a nightclub or rave together. Slowly, we grew our community, and our building became the hub for not only our own friends but also friends of our friends. Without realizing it, we'd created and developed our own tribe, and the most common meeting point became the loft that I lived in.

As our group grew, I realized that forming new friendships and deepening the connections within our burgeoning tribe was bringing both a sense of stability and a sense of excitement about the future for all of us. The connectedness we felt was making all of us happier, and we realized that it was something that we had all missed from our college days. It was something that, like many people, we had unwittingly lost upon graduating from college, and we didn't realize how much we missed it until we accidentally re-created it for ourselves.

I made a note to myself to make sure I never lost sight of the value of a tribe where people truly felt connected and cared about the well-being of one another. To me, connectedness—the number and depth of my relationships—was an important element of my happiness, and I was grateful for our tribe. The purpose of my big birthday party coming up wasn't actually meant to focus on me. My birthday was just the excuse. The party I had been planning for months was going to be my gift to the tribe.

Ever since selling LinkExchange, I'd committed to living by the philosophy that experiences were much more important to me than material things. Most people assumed that I would have gone out and bought a fancy and expensive car, but I was content with my Acura Integra.

I already lived in a fourteen-hundred-square-foot loft on the seventh floor of our building, and I had found out a few months earlier that a thirty-five-hundred-square-foot penthouse unit on the eighth floor was available for sale. It was unit number 810.

I had no desire to move, but when I saw the layout of the 810 loft, I knew I had to buy it so that it could become the new gathering space for our tribe. There was one small bedroom and three thousand square feet of wide-open space. It was the perfect place for partying.

I bought the 810 loft, not because I wanted to own more property, and not because I thought of it as a real estate investment. I bought 810 so I could architect our parties and gatherings. Owning the loft would ultimately enable more experiences.

After successfully buying 810 in a bidding war against two other people, I started working on converting the loft into my vision of what it could one day become. During college, watching the hit TV show *Friends* with my roommates was a regular weekly event. I remembered how the characters in the show seemed to always gather at the local coffee shop called Central Perk to hang out and meet other people. I wanted 810 to become our tribe's own private version of Central Perk. And we needed to figure out a cool name for 810, instead of just calling it 810.

I envisioned our friends gathering in 810 on Sundays for champagne brunches. I envisioned 810 as being the afterparty meet-up spot after a night out at a club, bar, or rave. And I envisioned converting 810 into our own private nightclub. The first official party of 810 would be on Saturday, December 11, 1999. At midnight, I would turn twenty-six. My birthday would be the perfect excuse to throw an inaugural party for 810.

I made sure to stock plenty of Red Bull.

I'd spent weeks preparing for my birthday party. Our tribe had attended several raves in the months leading up to my birthday. I remember the first rave party I had attended earlier that year, when I didn't really know what a rave was. All I knew was they played a lot of techno and house music. I had gone to nightclubs before where they played the same type of music that they played at raves,

and I remember finding that music really annoying and not understanding why the biggest rooms in all the clubs always seemed to
play that type of music. There were no words to the music, and it
seemed like it was just the same repetitive beat playing over and
over again incessantly. I just didn't understand the appeal of electronic music.

Knowing that it would be the same type of music, I wasn't too
excited about going to a warehouse rave, but because everyone else
in our tribe wanted to go, I decided to tag along.

We all drove to a gigantic empty warehouse that seemed like it
was in the middle of nowhere. There were hundreds of cars parked
outside the warehouse, and we could hear the repetitive thump-
ing of the electronic techno music as we waited outside in line. I
secretly wondered how long we would be staying there, as I would
have really preferred a venue with music that I recognized and had
heard on the radio. After waiting in line for twenty minutes, we
finally turned the corner and walked into the warehouse.

What I experienced next changed my perspective forever.

Streams of giant green laser beams were shooting throughout
the entire warehouse, which was the size of ten football fields. Fog
machines helped create a sense of dreamlike surrealism as everyone
faced the DJ and moved in unison to the beat of the music. Cans
of Red Bull were strewn everywhere, and ultraviolet black lights
caused the fluorescent decorations on the walls and ceilings to glow
as if they were alien plants transported from another universe.

But it wasn't just about the decorations, or the black lights, or
the fog machines, or the lasers, or the massiveness of the warehouse. Something else about the scene and moment elicited an
emotional response from my entire being that was completely
unexpected, and I couldn't really place my finger on exactly what it
was or why I felt that way.

I tried to analyze what was different about this scene compared with the nightclub scene that I was more accustomed to. Yes, the decorations and lasers were pretty cool, and yes, this was the largest single room full of people dancing that I had ever seen. But neither of those things explained the feeling of awe that I was experiencing that was leaving me speechless. As someone who is usually known as being the most logical and rational person in a group, I was surprised to feel myself swept with an overwhelming sense of spirituality—not in the religious sense, but a sense of deep connection with everyone who was there as well as the rest of the universe.

There was a feeling of no judgment, and as I glanced around the warehouse, I saw each person as an individual to be appreciated for just being himself or herself, dancing to the music.

As I tried to analyze what was going on in more detail, I realized that the dancing here was different from the dancing I usually witnessed in nightclubs. Here, there was no sense of self-consciousness or feeling that anyone was dancing to be seen dancing, whereas in nightclubs, there was usually the feeling of being on display somehow. In nightclubs, people usually dance with each other. Here, it seemed that almost everyone was facing the same direction. Everyone was facing the DJ, who was elevated up on stage, as if he was channeling his energy to the crowd. It almost felt as if everyone was worshipping the DJ.

The entire room felt like one massive, united tribe of thousands of people, and the DJ was the tribal leader of the group. People weren't dancing to the music so much as the music seemed like it was simply moving through everyone. The steady wordless electronic beats were the unifying heartbeats that synchronized the crowd. It was as if the existence of individual consciousness had disappeared and been replaced by a single unifying group consciousness, the same way a flock of birds might seem like a single entity instead of a collection of individual birds. Everyone in the warehouse had a shared purpose. We were all contributors to the collective rave experience.

I didn't know it at the time, but ten years later I would learn that research from the field of the science of happiness would confirm that the combination of physical synchrony with other humans and being part of something bigger than oneself (and thus losing momentarily a sense of self) leads to a greater sense of happiness, and that the rave scene was simply the modern-day version of similar experiences that humans have been having for tens of thousands of years.

In the moment though, I felt a sense of experiential epiphany. It swept through my entire being. In that instant, I suddenly understood the appeal of the techno music. I couldn't simply listen to it the way I listened to music on the radio. I had to let it flow through me in the context of a mind-set that I hadn't really experienced until just now. It was like someone had bestowed on me the Rosetta Stone of techno music, and no amount of verbal explanation would have helped me understand it. I had to experience it for myself.

And in that one instant, I did. I had awakened. I had been transformed.

Finally, after all these years, I understood what the music was all about.

Vision

Our tribe ended up going to a lot more raves together. Some were massive, with thousands and thousands of people. Some were small with only fifty. I learned more about the rave community and culture. I learned that *PLUR* was an acronym that stood for "Peace, Love, Unity, Respect," and that it was the mantra for how people were supposed to carry themselves and behave both at raves and in life.

At raves, it was part of the culture and considered perfectly normal to approach complete strangers and strike up a conversation. Unlike the bar or nightclub scene, where that type of behavior is typically used by guys to try to pick up girls, at raves people were genuinely interested in getting to know each other as just people with no ulterior motive.

The idea of PLUR and the rave culture rubbed off on me beyond the rave scene. To me, it was really more a philosophy about always being open to meeting people no matter how they looked or what their backgrounds were. Every interaction with anyone anywhere was an opportunity to gain additional perspective. We are all human at the core, and it can be easy to lose sight of that in a world ruled by business, politics, and social status. The rave culture was a reminder that it was possible for the world to be a better place, for people to simply be appreciative of the humanity in one another.

I learned to feel comfortable starting conversations with complete strangers no matter where I was or who they were. I wound up writing about how I applied this strategy to business in Ivanka Trump's book *The Trump Card: Playing to Win in Work and Life*.

My Excerpt for Ivanka Trump's Book

I personally really dislike "business networking" events. At almost every one of these events, it seems like the goal is to walk around and find people to trade business cards with, with the hope of meeting someone who can help you out in business and in exchange you can help that person out somehow. I generally try to avoid those types of events, and I rarely carry any business cards around with me.

Instead, I really prefer to focus on just building relationships and getting to know people as just people, regardless of their position in the business world or even if they're not from the business world. I believe that there's something interesting about anyone and everyone—you just have to figure out what that something is. If anything, I've found that it's more interesting to build relationships with people that are *not* in the business world because they almost always can offer unique perspectives and insights, and also because those relationships tend to be more genuine.

If you are able to figure out how to be truly interested in someone you meet, with the goal of building up a friendship instead of trying to get something out of that person, the funny thing is that almost always, something happens later down the line that ends up benefiting either your business or yourself personally.

I don't really know why this happens or why it works, but it seems that the benefit from getting to know someone on a personal level usually happens 2–3 years after you started working on building the relationship. And it's usually something that you could not have possibly predicted would have happened at the beginning of the relationship. For example, maybe your friend's sister's neighbor was just hired as the VP of a company that you've been trying to get in touch with, or maybe someone you met 2 years ago now has a new tennis partner who would be the perfect person for that job opening you've been trying to fill for the past 6 months.

Zappos.com has been around for over 10 years now. We grew from no sales in 1999 to over $1 billion in gross merchandise sales in 2008. In looking back at the major turning points in the history of the company, it seems that most of them were the result of pure luck. Things happened that we could not have possibly predicted, but they were the result of relationships that we had started building 2–3 years earlier.

So my advice is to stop trying to "network" in the traditional business sense, and instead just try to build up the number and depth of your friendships, where the friendship itself is its own reward. The more diverse your set of friendships are, the more likely you'll derive both personal and business benefits from your friendships later down the road. You won't know exactly what those benefits will be, but if your friendships are genuine, those benefits will magically appear 2–3 years later down the road.

I wanted my twenty-sixth birthday party to embody the same positive energy I'd experienced in the rave culture, so in the weeks leading up to it, I did everything I could to make sure it would be a night to remember. I went on an online shopping spree and ordered fog machines, colored lights, light controllers, lasers, disco balls, black lights, fluorescent decorations, and trusses to hang the lights and lasers on. I wanted to re-create a smaller version of the warehouse rave environment.

About a hundred people showed up for my birthday party. I had put up signs from the elevator that said "810" along with an arrow pointing toward the party loft. The cousin of one of the members of our tribe saw the sign and asked, "What's BIO?" The rest of us laughed. That was the name we were looking for. We decided to call the party loft "Club BIO" from that point forward.

For the most part, my birthday party went off without a hitch. The most important lesson I learned was to not serve grapes at a party, because the morning after, the entire kitchen floor was covered and stained with crushed grapes that had fallen onto the floor and been stepped on. It looked like I was running a vineyard inside Club BIO. I made a mental note to skip the fruit for my New Year's party.

Word of mouth spread quickly about Club BIO, and several hundred people showed up for my New Year's party. There was a line from the elevator to the entrance of the loft. By 3:00 AM, most of the partygoers had gone home. There were only about thirty people left, so I decided to crank up the output of the fog machines so that I could fill the entire loft with fog.

Suddenly, strobe lights flashed repeatedly as a loud, shrill alarm started sounding. It took me a while to figure out where the noise was coming from and what was going on: The dense output of the fog machines had set off the smoke alarms not just for my loft, but *for the entire building*. It was 3:00 AM, and the fire alarm was being sounded for all of the units. An automated voice announcement instructed everyone to evacuate the building immediately.

I quickly turned off the fog machines and opened all of the windows. The fog cleared after a few minutes, but by then it was too late. I heard the sound of sirens, and looked outside the windows to see two fire trucks approach the building with their lights flashing.

A few minutes later, three firemen showed up at the door. I explained to them what had happened, and showed them the lasers and fog machine setup. When they realized that the building was not actually in danger of burning down, they started laughing, wished all of us a happy New Year, and left the building. I was just happy that I wasn't arrested.

I breathed a sigh of relief and leaned out one of the open windows to watch the firemen get back into their fire trucks below. The lights of the fire trucks were still flashing.

Suddenly I heard a female voice. "Isn't this amazing? You created all of this."

I looked over to see who it was, but it was someone I didn't recognize. She had blond hair and blue eyes, and was also leaning out the window to marvel at the flashing lights of the fire trucks below.

"Yeah, they were pretty nice about it. I was worried that they would be mad at me, especially since it's New Year's," I said.

"That's not what I meant. I mean all of this," she said. She turned and gestured toward the rest of the people that were still at the party. "You could have done anything you wanted, and you chose to create an experience that people will remember forever."

"Yeah, I don't think other residents living here are going to be too happy with me when they find out why they had to evacuate the building in the middle of the night," I said. "They're probably going to remember this night forever as well."

She laughed. "Oh, don't worry about it. It was an accident. You can blame it on the Y2K bug or something. I can see the headlines now: Fog Machines Gone Awry!"

I smiled at her. "Can you believe that this whole place is going to be converted to an office in a few days?"

She gazed into my eyes. I could still hear the music in the background, but the rest of the world seemed to disappear. I had no idea who this girl was, but somehow the universe had brought us together for a single moment in time that I would remember forever.

"Envision, create, and believe in your own universe, and the universe will form around you," she said softly. "Just like what you did tonight."

She leaned over and whispered into my ear, "Happy New Year."

And then she got up and left, without another word.

Incubator

Her words stuck with me: "Envision, create, and believe in your own universe."

Although connecting with my new tribe of friends played a big role in increasing my level of happiness, I missed not actually being part of creating something. Just sitting on the sidelines and investing was boring. I wanted to be part of building something, and creating the Venture Frogs Incubator was an important piece to building my own universe.

In addition to signing the lease for the office space of our future incubator, Alfred and I also signed a lease for a restaurant in the same building, which we would call Venture Frogs Restaurant.

My parents had moved back from overseas and volunteered to run the Venture Frogs Restaurant over the next several years. The dishes in the restaurant were named after various dot-com companies. One of the crowd favorites ended up being the Akamai Fried Rice.

We had a restaurant, a gym, movie theaters, incubator office space, and lofts all under one roof. We hired a handful of employees to keep the incubator offices up and running.

We were creating our own universe.

With the Zappos crew moving into our building (initially into the converted party loft, and then eventually into the incubator office space), I started spending more and more time with the company.

The raves I went to slowly became more and more commercialized, and the events started feeling like they were more about making money than they were about spreading the PLUR culture. They started to attract a different type of crowd, and people's attitudes at the events started to shift. I realized that I had discovered raves at the tail end of the movement.

Without Club BIO as the party loft to serve as a central meet-up location, the tribe that we had built slowly started drifting apart. We had been bound by a common purpose in the beginning: to form a community. It was exciting in the early days, because every day we saw our tribe grow and strengthen.

But we lacked a shared purpose beyond just hanging out and partying. We still continued to keep in touch, but without something for us to make progress toward, and without a default meeting place that was the equivalent of Central Perk, different members of our tribe started focusing on other things that were going on in their lives. Some of us tried to figure out what our true passions were so that we would have something better than partying to focus on.

I was one of those people.

I had always been passionate about planning and throwing parties because I really enjoyed the idea of architecting and creating experiences and memories. I enjoyed watching people's reactions and hearing them say "WOW" when they walked into a party that was unlike any that they had ever been to. It was gratifying for people to come up to me at the end of the night or the next day and tell me what an incredible time they had.

But as passionate as I was about all of that, I didn't see party planning as a full-time occupation for me. I thought of it more as a hobby that I was passionate about, and I needed to find something more meaningful that I could dedicate myself to full-time.

They say that novelty is the biggest aphrodisiac. Making the initial investment to fund new ideas and companies was exciting, but in a relatively short period of time, Alfred and I had made twenty-seven investments and there was no more money left in the fund. Without more investment capital, we couldn't get involved with any new companies, and the excitement of being an investor wore off quickly.

At the time, almost every idea we heard seemed like a great idea, so the money went quickly. (We would find out ten years later that, on average, we had made a slight profit on most of the companies that we invested in, but the vast majority of the profits from the fund would come from Zappos. It turns out venture investing is a lot like poker. The one who makes the most money isn't the one who tries to play and win as many hands as possible. At the end of 2009, we had distributed over 5.8 times the initial fund amount to our investors, making Venture Frogs one of the top-performing funds from 1999.)

In April 2000, the high-flying dot-com stocks started to crash in the stock market, causing widespread panic throughout Silicon Valley. Many companies went out of business, and the venture-capital firms that we were counting on to take our portfolio companies to the next level scaled back and refused to provide additional funding for almost all of our investments.

A couple of companies moved into our new incubator office space, but without additional funding, they stopped paying their bills and went out of business a few months after that.

Eventually, Zappos was the only company left in the incubator, and we weren't optimistic about the prospects of any other companies moving in anytime soon. It was a bad situation for our fund, for the incubator, and for Zappos.

Alfred and I originally had the ambitious goal of raising a second fund of $100 million. We had done all the paperwork, and asked investors who had participated in our original fund if they wanted to put money into our second fund.

Our first fund had been a great vehicle for meeting a lot of interesting companies and people in a relatively short amount of time. As general managers of the fund, we had taken the idea of having the universe come to us and made it happen. We enjoyed learning about new companies, meeting new people, entertaining new ideas, and making new investments.

The problem was that once the investments had all been made, most of our time was spent dealing with companies that were not doing well and were unable to raise additional venture-capital money to keep them going.

We thought our best bet was to raise a second fund. If we could raise $100 million, then we could provide the next round of funding for the portfolio companies from our first fund to get them to the next level.

We sent out an e-mail to our previous investors to get an idea of how many would be interested in participating, and then waited anxiously for their response.

As it turned out, not a single person was interested. We ended up raising exactly $0.

Up until this point, I hadn't been too worried about the dot-com crash. Even though LinkExchange had been a bad experience from a culture perspective, financially it was a success story. Alfred and I had used our credibility from the LinkExchange sale to raise the $27 million for our first fund, so we naturally assumed that it wouldn't be that hard to raise money for our second fund.

We were wrong.

I started to have feelings of self-doubt. I wondered whether I had just gotten lucky with LinkExchange. Was I just a dot-com lottery winner who happened to be at the right place at the right time?

Alfred and I had continued to keep in touch with Michael Moritz at Sequoia about Zappos, and despite the progress that Zappos was making, Sequoia was still not interested in investing.

I believed with all my heart that Zappos had a great shot at succeeding. I felt that I needed to prove to myself and to Sequoia that the financial success of LinkExchange was not a fluke, that it wasn't just dumb luck. I wanted to prove to the world that I could do it again.

So I decided to take off my investor and adviser hat and put on my entrepreneur hat again. I joined Zappos full-time later that year. I decided that Zappos was going to be the universe that I wanted to help envision and build. It would be the universe that I believed in.

My search over the past few months was finally at an end. I had figured out what I wanted to focus on for at least the next few years. I had discovered my new passion.

I was passionate about proving everyone wrong.

Tweets to Live By

- "A great company is more likely to die of indigestion from too much opportunity than starvation from too little."
  —Packard's Law

- "You can't stop the waves, but you can learn to surf."
  —Jon Kabat-Zinn

- "Told ghost stories w/friends last night. Now wondering whether ghosts sit around campfires & tell each other People Stories?"

- "To dare is to lose one's footing momentarily. To not dare is to lose oneself."

  —Søren Kierkegaard

- Be humble: "In the beginner's mind there are many possibilities, but in the expert's mind there are few."

  —Shunryu Suzuki

PROFITS AND PASSION

4

Concentrate Your Position

Figuring Things Out

The next two years were stressful at Zappos. We were just focused on survival. We knew we had no choice but to succeed. We went through a recession, the dot-com stock market crash, and 9/11. At every turn, it felt like the universe was testing our commitment and our passion.

We knew we couldn't raise any funding externally. Although it went against our investment strategy, since I was now personally working full-time at Zappos, Alfred and I decided to invest some more money from the Venture Frogs fund, but eventually we had used up what little money was left in the fund.

Because the fund was out of money, every few months, I would take a look at my own bank account and personally put a little bit more money into the company in order to keep it afloat.

Alfred and I continued to try to reach out to Sequoia, but they still weren't interested in investing. In October 2000, I sent the following e-mail out stressing the importance of getting the company to profitability before we ran out of cash and cutting back on a lot of the things that we wanted to do.

Date: October 19, 2000
From: Tony Hsieh
To: Zappos Employees
Subject: 9-Month Plan
Zapponians:

I just wanted to send out an email to everyone about our company priorities over the next 9 months so that everyone can get a better idea of how different people's roles fit into the big picture. If you have any questions, please feel free to ask!

As you all know, the market has been pretty bad over the past 6 months for business-to-consumer (B2C) companies, both in the public markets and in the private (VC) markets. Once high-flying public companies such as eToys, Fogdog, PlanetRx are at all-time lows. High-profile private companies such as Miadora.com, which was doing $1 million a month in revenue and was funded by Sequoia (funders of Yahoo!), have gone out of business because VCs are afraid to fund B2C companies now.

These market conditions have been both good and bad for Zappos.com. On the positive side, it means that we don't have to worry about a competitor suddenly getting $25 million in funding and spending it on Super Bowl ads, confusing the marketplace, and in general giving us a lot of short-term headaches. On the downside, it means that, because we are constrained by cash, we won't be able to grow as quickly as we'd like to or do all the things we'd like to.

And there are a lot of things that would be nice for us to do if we had the money, such as doing a national ad campaign, growing our customer service and fulfillment team more quickly, spending more on development resources, putting more features into the new site, and much, much more. But the reality is that, at this time, we can't do everything we want to do because of cash constraints.

Right now, because we are unprofitable with very limited cash, we are in a race against time. Our number one priority as a company right now is to get to the other side: Once we are profitable, we are in control of our own destiny, and can start doing a lot more of the things that we would like to do.

Until that time, we need to make sure that as a company, we stay focused on maximizing our chances of getting to profitability before we run out of money. We have a financial plan in place that makes sense and is within our reach of accomplishing, but we have to make sure that we all understand what's required in order to follow the plan.

So, first and foremost, we need to watch our expenses very carefully. We have a budget set aside for hiring which will need to be followed very carefully, and we won't be able to hire as many people as we'd like in any of our departments.

After watching expenses, our most important priority is to maximize the gross profit we make over the next 9 months. This translates into increasing the average gross profit and order size per customer, increasing conversion rates, increasing new qualified visitors to our site, and increasing the percentage of repeat customers.

In evaluating new projects for the company over the next 9 months, we need everyone to think about how it will increase our total gross profit over the next 9 months. This will mean that some projects that we might normally pursue will have to be put on hold until we get to profitability. Once we get to profitability, then we will be able to think longer-term and bigger picture, and fantasize more about how to rule the world.

As I mentioned above, if anyone has any questions about how things fit into our 9-month plan, please don't hesitate to ask.

We knew that just harping on the urgency of the situation wasn't going to be enough. We had to take more drastic measures.

Nick, Fred, and I decided to do a round of layoffs in order to maximize our chances of survival. And we had to figure out how to get the remaining employees to either take big pay cuts or work for free in exchange for equity in the company. My salary was set to $24 a year, or $1 per paycheck (although that was before taxes).

In November 2000, Nick sent me this e-mail:

Date: November 26, 2000
From: Nick Swinmurn
To: Tony Hsieh
Subject: Stuff

I don't have any input on funding. Unfortunately seems like you are only option so I guess you need to decide what makes sense for you and then we react accordingly. If you don't have more money for Zappos then we should look at what we have left and figure out now how we can make last as long as possible with skeleton crew.

As for me taking another pay cut, once my old landlord admits he owes me more money and I sell a few things to a friend, I should be completely out of debt leaving only costs as rent, car and food. Biggest wildcard is rent/deposit. As long as pay covers my costs I'll be fine.

I think even though we still have problems we are on right track. Marketing is now close to a proper percent of revenue, technically are much more efficient, and seem to know what needs to happen for it to work. Frustrating because I think we all know we can make it, just question of if we can survive long enough.

Other employees came up with creative solutions:

After carefully considering the choices, I have decided not to switch to any of the alternate packages offered. However, I recognize that Zappos wants (needs?) to trim back on spending, so I have a counter offer. The main thing I am interested in right now is expanding my personal time. I'd be willing to take a 20% pay cut in exchange for one extra day per week off.

As things started to look more and more bleak, some people decided to leave the company. Most employees didn't have any savings, so taking a big pay cut or working for free meant that they wouldn't able to pay their rent, so we racked our brains trying to come up with more creative solutions.

The party loft I had was actually empty now that Zappos had moved into the incubator offices, so I put five beds in 810 (formerly Club BIO) and started housing employees there without charging them rent.

I also owned three other lofts in the building and housed some incubator and Zappos employees (including Nick) in there as well, and also let them live there without charging rent. Of the people remaining, we lived by an "all-for-one, one-for-all" credo and did everything we could to keep the company afloat.

Everyone remaining stepped up and worked harder than before, and we were pleasantly surprised to find that the layoffs actually didn't hurt the company's productivity. We realized that we had laid off the underperformers and the nonbelievers, but because everyone remaining was so passionate about the company and believed in what we were doing, we could still accomplish just as much work as we had before.

It was a big lesson in the power of instilling passion throughout the entire company and working as a unified team. Everyone was making sacrifices.

But it still wasn't enough to get us to profitability.

I continued to put some of my own personal cash into the company every few months, but I knew it wasn't sustainable. The company was still losing too much cash every month.

As the money in my personal bank account started dwindling away, I began selling the real estate that I owned so that I could put the proceeds from each sale back into Zappos. I eventually ended up selling every property I had bought except for the one I lived in and the party loft. I had wanted to sell the party loft, but the economy was so bad that there simply were no interested buyers.

On top of that, the restaurant that my parents were running was not meeting its sales projections, in part due to the economy and in part because none of us had any restaurant experience.

The situation was dire. Everything I was involved in was running out of money, including the restaurant, the incubator, Zappos, and myself personally.

The only backup plan I had for myself personally was the thought that, whenever the economy would eventually turn around, I would be able to sell the party loft and convert that to cash. That would be my cushion and safety net, although I had no idea when the economy would eventually turn around or how long it would take to sell a loft like that.

Nick, Fred, and I looked at other areas in the business where we could try to cut expenses. Even though it would hurt our growth, we decided to cut most of our marketing expenses, and refocused our efforts on trying to get the customers who had already bought from us to purchase again and more frequently. Little did we know that this was actually a blessing in disguise, as it forced us to focus more on delivering better customer service. In 2003, we would decide to make customer service the focus of the company.

Even so, at the time, our number one priority wasn't customer service. It was simply survival.

The need to survive and figure things out had an unanticipated consequence. It brought all of us closer together because we all shared the same goal of not going out of business. Even though we were going through some tough times, we were going through everything together, and we were all fiercely passionate about what we were doing. We had all made sacrifices in our own way because we all believed in the potential and future of the company.

Without realizing it, Zappos had become my new tribe.

Believe

Looking at the company's financials, it became pretty clear that just focusing on cutting expenses wasn't going to get the company to profitability. We needed to figure out a way to grow sales.

This was a particularly challenging problem because we had cut back most of our marketing budget. We were already focusing more on getting the customers we already had to shop with us more often, but that alone wouldn't get us very far in the short term.

What we really needed was a miracle.

In high school, I'd taken a Greek history class and learned about *deus ex machina,* which is a Latin phrase that literally translates into "god from the machine." According to Wikipedia, it is a "plot device in which a person or thing appears out of the blue to help a character overcome a seemingly insolvable difficulty. It is generally considered to be a poor storytelling technique."

As I sat in the office at my desk pondering what to do next, I turned to Fred. I didn't care if this would make for a bad story later as long as we could figure out how to save the company.

"Fred, do you have a *deus ex machina?*" I asked.

"A what?" Fred was confused.

"Deus ex machina," I repeated. "You know, a Greek miracle."

"Oh, no, sorry," he replied. "I accidentally left mine at home in my shirt pocket."

"Maybe we can find one over a drink," I said. "It's 4:00 PM and we need to figure out how to save the company. Is it too early for a drink?"

"Of course not."

So we stopped what we were doing and headed over to the bar at Venture Frogs Restaurant. I ordered a Grey Goose soda and Fred ordered a beer. We sipped our drinks in silence for a few minutes.

I broke the ice. "So . . . any ideas on how to increase sales more quickly?"

Fred looked pensive. "I come from a merchandising background. I like to say that all we need is the right product at the right time in the right quantity, and the sales will take care of themselves. The problem is that we don't carry the brands or the styles that I know will sell. We just don't have the right products to offer our customers."

"How do we get the right products?"

"The problem is that a lot of the brands that we want to carry can't drop ship," Fred said. "Their systems and warehouses aren't set up to send the orders from their warehouse directly to our customers. And even for the brands that can drop ship, usually they're sold out of their best stuff, so we wouldn't be able to offer those styles to our customers."

I paused for a moment to think about what Fred was saying. "So how come all the brick-and-mortar stores are able to offer all the best-selling brands and styles?" I asked.

"Because they hold and own the inventory," Fred explained. "The brick-and-mortar retailers future out their orders ahead of time, pay for the inventory, and take the inventory risk. If a retailer isn't able to sell something, then that's the retailer's problem, not the brand's or wholesaler's problem. But we can't do that, because that's not our business model."

We had both finished our drinks.

"Another drink?" I asked. Fred nodded solemnly and motioned for the bartender to bring us another round.

"So... what if we did that?" I said, thinking out loud. "What if we carried all the inventory of the brands and styles you wanted? How much do you think our sales would go up by?"

"Oh, we'd easily triple sales, no question," Fred said without hesitation. "Probably even more than that."

"Okay, let's figure out what we need to do to make that happen. If changing our business model is what's going to save us, then we need to embrace and drive change."

Fred and I spent the next hour talking through all the different challenges that we would have to address if we wanted to start carrying inventory in addition to the drop shipping business that we were already doing. By the end of the hour, we felt we had a pretty good list. The list was daunting, but at least we now knew what we needed to do to save the company:

1) We would need to hire and grow a buying team to decide what products to buy and to manage the inventory. Fred could do this in the short term, but at some point we would need a dedicated team.

2) We would still need to convince the brands to sell to us. Most of the brands that we wanted would only sell to brick-and-mortar stores.

3) We would need to update our software to enable our Web site to sell inventoried products instead of just products that were being drop shipped.

4) We would need a warehouse to hold all the inventory we were buying. We would need to hire staff to ship the shoes out of our warehouse.

5) To address number 2, we would need to open up a physical retail store and hire staff to actually run it. Given our current financial situation, it would be pretty hard to convince any landlord to sign a lease with us.

6) We would have to figure out how to come up with the cash to purchase the inventory we wanted. Fred figured we would need another $2 million. The problem was that we didn't have an extra $2 million lying around.

7) We would have to accomplish all of these things within a few months.

Fred and I divided up the list. He would handle numbers 1 and 2. I would work with our computer programmers and work on number 3. For 4, we figured we could get everyone in the office to squeeze together and turn half of the office into our warehouse for the short term.

"What about number 5?" Fred asked. "How are we going to open up a brick-and-mortar store?"

"What if we turned the reception area of our office into a 'store'?" I asked. "What's the definition of a store? What if stuff is available for purchase but we end up selling only one pair of shoes a week out of the store, and the rest off the Internet? Does that still count as a brick-and-mortar store?"

"I guess technically that would fit the definition of a store. Some of the brands might go for it, but probably not most of them once they saw what the store looked like," Fred said.

"Well, let's start with that then," I said. "And in the meantime, we can start looking for a real store that's in some small town somewhere that doesn't do a lot of business. We can buy the store for cheap if it's in the middle of nowhere. And once we take that store over, then all of the brands that the store is carrying can be grandfathered to us as the new owners of the store. We can start selling those brands on our Web site at that point."

Fred looked skeptical. "I guess it doesn't hurt to try asking around. What's the worst that can happen? All they can do is say no.

"But what about number 6?" Fred went on. "Where are we going to get the money to pay for all the inventory for the new brands we sign up?"

I looked at him. "I'll worry about that part. Just assume that if you can convince a brand to sell to us, then we'll have the money to pay for the inventory for that brand."

I had no idea how Fred was going to convince enough brands to work with us in such a short period of time, and Fred had no idea how I was going to come up with the cash to pay for the inventory. But we trusted each other, and we knew we were in this together. This was a "bet-the-company" plan. Our new strategy was going to either save Zappos or ensure our speedy demise. But we really had no other option. Continuing with the drop-ship-only route that we had been on and dying a slow death didn't sound like very much fun. It would just be delaying the inevitable.

What Fred didn't know was that while we were talking, I had already formulated a plan for getting the $2 million. But I didn't want to tell Fred what I was thinking, because he probably wouldn't have gone along with it. My plan was to take almost everything that I had left in my name and liquidate it in a fire sale. I would bet the farm and put all the proceeds into Zappos. To an outsider, it may have seemed like a desperate and reckless plan.

But in my mind, it wasn't. We had taken Zappos this far, and there was no turning back now. In my heart, I knew it was the right thing to do.

I believed in Zappos, and I believed in Fred.

Improvising Inventory

Fred started making calls to the brands we wanted, and we converted our reception area into a mini shoe store. Since we were in the same building as a movie theater, I'm pretty sure that the moviegoers thought we were crazy. A shoe store in the lobby area of a fourteen-screen movie theater complex just wasn't something people expected to see as they handed their tickets to the usher. It was a little weird.

But it worked.

As soon as our first shipment came in, sales on our Web site started picking up. True to his word, Fred signed up more and more brands, and within a few months the shoes were taking up more of our office space than the people were. The maximum capacity for our offices was about five thousand pairs of shoes, and we were quickly running out of space.

Fred had asked around and found a small mom-and-pop shoe store in a tiny town called Willows about two hours north of our offices. The owner was looking to retire, and we ended up buying the business for a small amount of cash. Suddenly, we had access to a lot more brands whose products we could inventory, and our sales started to skyrocket.

As luck would have it, there was an abandoned building across the street that used to be a department store. We took a look at it and figured it would be able to hold about fifty thousand pairs of shoes—ten times more than our current capacity—so we ended up renting out that space as well. We moved our inventory from San Francisco to Willows and started hiring employees there to run our new warehouse.

Fred was right. By a lot. Our sales did much more than just triple. In 2000, we did about $1.6 million in gross merchandise sales. In 2001, we ended up doing $8.6 million in gross merchandise sales. Our growth rate surprised even ourselves, and everyone was excited about our new business model, which combined drop shipping with selling inventoried products.

Even though our sales were up, we still weren't cash-flow-positive because we had to pay for all the extra inventory that we were buying in order to fuel our sales growth. But we knew we were on the right path.

In early 2002, a company called eLogistics approached us. The salesman told us that they had a warehouse in Kentucky located right next to the UPS Worldport hub. The salesman told us that they could handle all of our fulfillment operations, so we wouldn't need to worry about running a warehouse ourselves. But more importantly, by relocating our warehouse in Kentucky, we would be able to cut our shipping expenses and get our orders to our customers faster.

We had been shipping out of California, which meant that ground shipments to the East Coast were taking as long as seven or eight days. By shipping out of a more central state such as Kentucky, we would be able to reach 70 percent of our customers within two days by UPS ground. It seemed like a win–win scenario: It was good for our customers, and it was good for our bottom line. The faster shipping would be a way for us to WOW our customers through better service.

We signed on with eLogistics and started putting together a plan for transferring all of our inventory in the Willows warehouse over to the eLogistics warehouse. It was going to require a lot of careful coordination, because it would take three days for all the trucks to drive across the country. Our plan was to pack everything into the trucks on a Friday, but keep the Web site up and running so we wouldn't lose any sales. The trucks would arrive by Sunday, get unloaded and moved into the eLogistics warehouse by end of day Monday, and then on Tuesday we would ship out the orders that had been placed by customers over the weekend.

We planned down to the last detail to make sure everything would go smoothly, and on Friday we sent most of our San Francisco employees to Willows to help with packing the trucks. We had to pack forty thousand pairs of shoes into five semitrailer trucks as quickly as possible. It was a big task, but everyone came together and made it happen. The last truck left at 5:00 PM.

Fred and I were happy that things went off without a hitch, because we had planned on going on a short vacation together along with our significant others.

Twenty-four hours later, we were in New Orleans, exploring the world-famous Bourbon Street. The move had been stressful, and we were glad that all the planning had paid off. We could finally relax for a little bit.

Or so we thought.

A day into our mini vacation, I received a phone call from eLogistics.

"Tony, I have some bad news. One of the trucks drove off the road and overturned. The driver is in the hospital, but he'll be okay. The shoes are strewn all over the side of the highway. I don't think we'll be able to recover any of them."

This was bad. We had just lost 20 percent of our inventory, which we estimated was worth about $500k at retail. And, since we had continued to accept orders on our Web site, that meant we would have to contact 20 percent of those customers and tell them that they wouldn't be getting their shoes.

Fred and I spent the next few days on long phone calls coordinating with eLogistics and our employees, trying to sort everything out. We contacted our customers and told them what had happened. Some of them didn't believe us and threatened to report us to the Better Business Bureau. We ended up figuring things out in the end, but it put a bit of a damper on our trip.

I tried to look on the bright side of things. I had another trip coming up in a couple of months and I still had that to look forward to.

Back in 2001, my friend Jenn and I had planned on going on a three-week trip to Africa. I had first met Jenn at my birthday party in the party loft. Even though we wouldn't consider ourselves to be outdoorsy people or especially athletic, we decided that we wanted to hike and summit Mount Kilimanjaro, the tallest peak in all of Africa. Our original trip had been planned for October 2001, but after the 9/11 attacks, we decided to postpone it until July of the following year.

For me, summiting the tallest mountain of a continent was one of those things that I wanted to check off of my list of things to do at some point in my life. It went with my life philosophy of valuing experiences over things. Jenn had originally proposed the trip because she had recently been laid off from her dot-com consulting job and wanted to use the opportunity to get away.

In the weeks leading up to the trip, we spent our weekends running around trying to get ready. We bought our hiking gear, got our immunization shots, and made sure our passports and travel visas were all taken care of.

*   *   *

Meanwhile, it was getting stressful back at Zappos. Things weren't going well at eLogistics. The salesman had oversold their capabilities, and a lot of our customers weren't getting what they had ordered. From a company-survival point of view, though, what was even worse was that as more and more pallets of new shoes that we had ordered were showing up in our new warehouse, the eLogistics staff wasn't able to put them away in a timely manner. They had never had to deal with so many different types of brands, styles, sizes, and widths, so we had mountains and mountains of shoes just sitting on the loading dock that weren't being put away or scanned into our system.

This meant that we couldn't offer any of those items on our Web site. We calculated that we were losing tens of thousands of dollars' worth of sales every day that the shoes just sat unopened and unsorted on the loading dock.

We knew we had to do something fast when we learned about the situation, so Fred decided to call Keith. I'd first met Keith in 1996, when he was visiting the house of my apartment manager at the time. He was working as a mechanic for United Airlines.

When Alfred and I opened up the Venture Frogs Incubator, we hired Keith as our facilities manager, but like everyone else at Venture Frogs and Zappos, he ended up doing much more than what his job title suggested. He did whatever needed to be done. Keith eventually joined Zappos full-time and always volunteered to do anything from packing boxes to wiring up our phone systems to helping set up and run our warehouse in Willows.

When Fred called Keith, he was still at our Willows warehouse helping clean everything up now that the entire place had been emptied.

"Keith, we have a problem in Kentucky with eLogistics," Fred said. "It's a mess down there, we need someone from Zappos to help get all our inventory checked in."

"What do you need me to do?" Keith asked.

"How far are you from the Sacramento airport?"

"About an hour."

"There's a flight that leaves in two hours. We need you to head to the airport right now to catch the next flight to Kentucky," Fred said.

"Are you serious?"

"Yes."

"Um, can I go home and pack and leave tomorrow morning?" Keith asked.

"We can't afford to lose a single day. We're losing tens of thousands of dollars every day that passes. When you get to Kentucky, go buy some underwear and whatever else you need."

"Um. All right. How long do I need to be out there?"

"Until we get this figured out," Fred said. "Probably a week, maybe two. We should stop talking so you don't miss your flight."

"Okay."

Keith hung up and drove straight to the airport. During his drive, he made a phone call to arrange for someone to take care of his dog while he was gone.

How's Keith doing?" I asked Fred. A week had passed since Keith had dropped everything on a moment's notice and hopped onto a plane to Kentucky.

"I just talked to him," Fred said. "He says everything at eLogistics is a mess. It's a bigger problem than we all thought, and he's going to have to stay there for at least a few more weeks."

"Wow, that's a long time. Did he go out and buy some clothes?"

"Yeah, he went to Wal-Mart and bought a bunch of stuff," Fred said. "Keith's a go-getter, though, he'll figure out how to fix what's going on there. But we have a problem on our end. We have less than two months of cash left. Are we going to be able to get more money to pay for all the inventory?"

"I'm working on it. I put the party loft up for sale, but haven't gotten any offers yet. But I just told my real estate agent to drop the price by 40 percent so hopefully we'll get some offers," I said.

"Are you sure you want to do that?" Fred gulped. "You're going to take a huge loss on that. I feel bad."

"Yeah, but it'll be worth it in the long run," I said. "I can either let the property sit around, and maybe five years from now it'll get back up to the price I paid for it. Or I can sell it now and invest the money into Zappos. I think Zappos will be worth at least ten times as much in five years, so I'll come out ahead. Don't feel bad. We're going to make this work."

I tried to say everything with as much confidence as possible, in part to try to convince myself as well. But the truth was, it was one of the most stressful times in my life.

It had ultimately been my decision to move our inventory to eLogistics, and I was worried that I had made the wrong call. There were no guarantees that I'd be able to sell the party loft before Zappos ran out of money. I was in a race against time.

I thought that there couldn't be a worse possible time to go climb a mountain in Africa, where there would be little or no access to phone or Internet. I thought about canceling the trip, but I realized that there really wasn't anything I could do to increase the chances of the party loft selling if I was around. Instead, I left standing instructions with my dad to accept any offer that came in for the party loft that was enough to pay for all the inventory and keep Zappos from going out of business in two months.

"I'll try to see if I can find a place to check e-mail after I'm down from the mountain," I said to Fred. "Can you send me an update on what's going on with eLogistics next Friday?"

Fred nodded.

In my head, I thought about what our options would be if eLogistics didn't work out. We would either need to find another warehouse service provider or set up a warehouse of our own out in Kentucky, in which case we'd have to find another building and negotiate a new lease. We would have to move all our inventory again. And all of this was dependent on the party loft selling, or else the company would be out of business. In the meantime, I hoped Fred would be able to convince more brands to sell to us so that we could increase our sales, but that would only help things if the new inventory we got didn't wind up just sitting on the loading docks. I thought through what seemed like a thousand "what-if" scenarios as I tried to answer as many e-mails as I could before I had to leave for my trip. I was in the middle of an e-mail when I realized that I had to stop typing.

I had a plane to catch.

Snows of Kilimanjaro

It was raining on the day that Jenn and I started hiking up Kilimanjaro. After flying from airport to airport for twenty-four hours, we had finally arrived in Tanzania. With a day of rest, we were driven to the drop-off point with all of our hiking gear and introduced to our guide and the rest of the team that would be navigating us up the mountain.

Although we were halfway around the world, I couldn't get Zappos out of my head. I knew that back at home, it felt like vultures were circling around Zappos. We had gotten so far, and had so much opportunity in front of us. But the cash flowing out of the company felt like an infection that overshadowed everything else that was going right. We could have prevented it if we had figured things out earlier, or if I hadn't bought the party loft in the first place. But now, the fate of the company rested on being able to find a buyer for the loft in time.

I'd already played out the scenario of what would happen if

there was no buyer, if things didn't work out. I told myself I would be at peace with it because it had been challenging, and a lot of fun, while it lasted. I was mentally and emotionally tired.

I thought about all the people over the past few years who had been a part of the adventure.

Our first day hiking Kilimanjaro was through dense rain forest. Although it was warm at first, the temperature had cooled down by the end of the day, and I was shivering from being soaked by the rain.

I was physically exhausted but I couldn't sleep, so I started imagining things in a dreamlike state. I was surprised to hear my cell phone ringing in the middle of the night. I had thought that there wouldn't be any reception this high up on the mountain.

It was my real estate agent, calling to tell me the good news: There was an offer for the party loft for more than the asking price. I immediately accepted, and then hung up. A sense of relief passed over me. We had made it over the hump. Zappos was saved.

Suddenly, the hiking that I had to do over the next five days didn't seem to be that big a deal anymore. Instead of hiking, I felt as if I was going to get on a rescue plane the next morning that would fly over the top of the snowcapped mountain and land me safely on the other side.

I slept peacefully for a few hours.

Then suddenly, I jolted awake. I thought I had heard an animal making a strange noise outside, but it turned out to be just a figment of my imagination.

And then a sinking feeling came over me as I realized the truth.

There was no phone call. There was no offer.

The whole conversation had been a dream.

Summit

The next four days hiking up Kilimanjaro tested my physical, mental, and emotional strength. We hiked twelve hours a day, making our way through five different climate zones: rain forest, alpine heath, moorland, desert, and snow.

I ended up getting a cold, with a cough and runny nose. The dryness at higher elevations caused me to get a bloody nose. Half the time spent hiking was with tissue paper stuck in my nostrils, making breathing even more difficult. And even though I'd taken altitude sickness medication, the high altitude resulted in headache, vomiting, and diarrhea. I was only carrying a day pack, but my shoulder and back started acting up and spasming. Physically, it was the most grueling thing I had ever done. Mentally and emotionally, I kept thinking about Zappos. I wondered if I would be able to sell the party loft in time, and what to do if that didn't happen. There were no showers or bathrooms. I was pretty miserable, and there were many times when I thought about giving up and turning around.

On the night before the summit, we set up camp at 5:00 PM and tried to go to sleep at 8:00 PM because we had to start our final summit at midnight. Neither Jenn nor I could sleep because we were at such a high altitude, so we ended up just tossing and turning until 11:30 PM, when we had to get up out of our tents to get dressed and ready for the hike.

We started hiking at midnight so that we could get to the peak in time to see the sunrise. We had been hiking for almost a week now, but this final summit was much harder than the daytime hikes we had done before. It was pitch black, and our headlamps were only bright enough for us to see five feet ahead of us. There was no way to look ahead to see how much farther we had to go, or to look behind to see how far we had gone. There was no sense of progress as we slowly put one foot in front of the other. I thought to myself that this must be what solitary confinement feels like.

We were bundled in eight layers of clothing because of the cold, which made stopping to take a bio break an awkward and uncomfortable ten-minute ordeal.

The final summit hike was also much tougher than anything we had done before because of the high altitude. After each step forward, I had to pause to inhale and exhale three times to catch my breath before I could put my next foot forward. If it had been light out, it would have seemed like slow progress. In the dark, it just seemed like no progress. We all hiked in complete silence because it would have taken too much physical effort to talk.

I started trying to play mind games with myself. I knew the entire hike would take about six hours, but I had no concept of how much time had passed. I imagined that I was driving from my home in San Francisco down to my friend's house in Palo Alto, which was a forty-five-minute drive I had made many times. I imagined the landmarks and highway exits along the way, and started counting my steps. I imagined that every hundred steps would be equivalent to driving five minutes farther, and I visualized in my head the progress I was making toward Palo Alto. Once I eventually made it to Palo Alto, I would turn around and drive back up to San Francisco in my head.

After two round trips, I needed something else to keep me mentally busy. Even though I had come this far and knew I was close to the summit, I still thought about turning back. If I'd been alone, I'm sure I would have.

I hadn't showered or had a decent meal or good night's sleep in five days. I started thinking about all the things that I took for granted in life, and how much more I should appreciate the things I had. I imagined what a nice, warm hot shower would feel like. I thought about what eating at Mel's Diner would be like. I imagined how delicious a turkey melt would be, dipped in chicken noodle soup. I made a mental note and promised myself that I would order that as my first meal when I got back home.

I remember thinking that this entire experience was by far the hardest thing I had ever done in my life. It was testing every ounce of willpower I had.

After what seemed like an eternity, we finally reached the summit just as the sun was rising. I couldn't believe that we had actually done it. We were standing at the highest point in all of Africa, looking down at the clouds below us, with the sun directly in front of us, its rays welcoming us to the beginning of a new day. It didn't seem like this was something that humans were meant to experience, yet here we were.

In that moment, I thought to myself, *Anything is possible.*

Tears welled up in my eyes.

I was speechless.

I gave Jenn a hug.

We took a picture, and I checked Kilimanjaro off my list of things to do.

End of an Era

I was back in San Francisco two weeks later, eating my turkey melt dipped in chicken noodle soup at Mel's Diner as I had promised myself. It tasted better than I had remembered. I took my time eating, trying to savor each and every bite.

I felt like I'd been to hell and back, and I had a whole new appreciation of the comforts of living in modern Western society. Showering and indoor toilets felt like luxuries.

As I sat at Mel's eating my turkey melt, I thought about what to do about Zappos. We had about a month of cash left before we were out of business. While I was in Africa, an offer for the party loft had indeed come through, but then the buyer backed out at the last minute because a fortune-teller had told her that the *feng shui* of the place would not be good for her.

I couldn't help but laugh when my real estate agent told me the story. I couldn't believe that the fate of the entire company rested on the advice of a fortune-teller.

I told my real estate agent to lower the price again.

A couple weeks later, with only two weeks' worth of cash left at Zappos, I received an offer for 40 percent below the price that I had originally paid for the party loft. It would have been customary to spend some time negotiating, but I didn't have time. So I accepted the offer immediately, trying not to think about the huge loss I was taking on the property.

As I signed the paperwork, I also tried not to think about all the great times and parties that so many people had been a part of during the glory days of Club BIO. I tried not to think of the blond girl who was next to me at the window on New Year's, talking about the universe while we gazed down at the swirling lights of the fire trucks below.

Selling the party loft symbolized the end of an era for me. It was hard not to feel wistful and nostalgic. The loft had created so many experiences and memories for so many people.

As soon as the deal closed, I transferred the money to Zappos and felt an overwhelming sense of relief. We had bought ourselves another six months before we would need more cash.

My parents weren't particularly thrilled that I had put all of my money into Zappos. They asked me if I was sure that I wanted to give up all that money, and I told them I was.

Alfred told me, "As your friend and financial adviser, I'm advising you not to do it. It might pay off in the long run, but it's not worth the risk of being completely broke."

I thought about Fred, how he had taken the leap of faith when he first joined Zappos because he believed in what was possible. He had given up a great career, just bought a new house, and had kids to take care of. He had risked his entire life for the Zappos dream.

I told Alfred I was going to follow Fred's footsteps and do the same thing. We had taken it this far, and I wanted to see how far we could take Zappos. Even if Zappos failed, we would know that we had done everything we could to chase a dream we believed in.

Now we had another six months of runway to figure things out. We weren't sure exactly how we were going to do it, but I was absolutely sure of one thing.

I never wanted to have to deal with another fortune-teller again.

Kentucky

Now that we had some breathing room on the financial side of things, we had another fire to put out: our warehouse operations. What was supposed to be a quick one-week trip to Kentucky for Keith had extended through the entire summer.

Things were not going well with eLogistics, and we weren't very optimistic that they would get better anytime soon. Orders weren't being shipped accurately, and we still had a lot of inventory that was sitting on the loading docks not being scanned in and put on the shelves. After an operations manager at eLogistics told us that the salesperson who had sold us on eLogistics had oversold their capabilities, we knew we needed to figure out something else.

Keith started driving around Kentucky looking for an empty warehouse, and eventually found one off the side of the highway, about fifteen minutes away from the Louisville airport. He contacted the landlord and learned that they would be willing to lease us fifty thousand square feet of space, with the ability to expand.

Keith and I talked and decided that we needed to take control and run our own warehouse again. We couldn't rely on a third party like eLogistics to take care of our customers, so we signed the lease for the new warehouse.

With the signing of the new lease, Keith realized that he was going to have to be in Kentucky for a while, so he flew back to California to pick up some stuff from home (he hadn't been home since he first hopped on the plane a couple of months before) and borrow a printer and fax machine from our office. Keith also wanted to get his truck out to Kentucky, so I told him that I would drive it back to Kentucky with him and help set up our new warehouse.

I had no idea how long I would be in Kentucky, but making sure our warehouse operations were running smoothly was now the highest priority for the company. We needed to make sure our new warehouse was designed properly so that we could get all our inventory checked in within hours upon arrival and ship out customer orders as quickly and as accurately as possible.

There was a lot of work waiting for us in Kentucky, so Keith and I decided to drive from San Francisco to Kentucky as fast as we could. We took turns driving, stopping only for gas along the way. We settled into a routine and tried to be as efficient as possible. While one of us was sleeping, the other would drive until we were out of gas. Then, while filling the truck up with gas, we would run inside, go to the bathroom, buy some food and a couple of energy drinks, and switch places. Each driving shift ended up being about three hours long.

About twenty hours into our trip, both of us were getting pretty tired, but we didn't want to stop, so we started experimenting with different energy drinks, turning on the air-conditioning, and cranking up the music to keep whoever was driving awake.

During one of my naps, I woke up to see Keith's hair and face completely drenched with water. At first I thought he was sweating profusely.

"Are you okay?" I asked. "Why are you so wet?"

"Yeah, I'm fine," Keith replied. "I was splashing some water on my face to stay awake."

"It looks like a little bit more than a splash."

"Oh, yeah, the splashing wasn't really working so I decided to pour the entire bottle of water all over my head. I'm pretty awake now."

If I wasn't so tired I probably would have laughed out loud, but I went back to sleep because I knew my driving shift was coming up soon.

After thirty-six hours of nonstop driving, Keith and I finally got to Kentucky. We slept for twelve hours straight, and when we finally woke up, both of us felt like we had a really bad hangover from pounding so many energy drinks. We calculated that we had each downed the equivalent of eighteen Red Bulls in thirty-six hours. But we were ready to get to work—we had a new warehouse to start setting up.

We decided to name our new warehouse and the systems we would build for it WHISKY—WareHouse Inventory System in KentuckY.

We told the people at eLogistics that we had opened up our own warehouse because we weren't happy with the service levels we were getting from them. We told them that they still had a chance to keep our business, but we were going to have our WHISKY warehouse operations compete against their operations for shipping and inventory accuracy. Every week, if WHISKY outperformed eLogistics, then we would take ten thousand pairs of shoes out of eLogistics and move them over to the WHISKY warehouse.

The people at eLogistics weren't very happy about our plan, but it was hard for them to argue against the logic of it. Every week, WHISKY outperformed eLogistics. Within a month, we had moved completely out of the eLogistics warehouse and all of our shipments were coming out of WHISKY. We were finally in control of our business again. (We would later learn that we had definitely made the right decision: The entire eLogistics business eventually shut down.)

It was a valuable lesson. We learned that we should never

outsource our core competency. As an e-commerce company, we should have considered warehousing to be our core competency from the beginning. Outsourcing that to a third party and trusting that they would care about our customers as much as we would was one of our biggest mistakes. If we hadn't reacted quickly, it would have eventually destroyed Zappos.

I ended up staying in Kentucky for five months, living out of a small hotel room. Keith focused on the physical aspects of the warehouse (shelving, conveyors, electricity, hiring) while I focused on the technical aspects of it (computer programming, systems, process design). Neither of us had any background in warehouse operations. We were experimenting and figuring things out as we went. We quickly outgrew the fifty thousand square feet we were leasing and worked with the landlord to expand our space.

As the end of 2002 neared, it was time for me to head back home. Our new warehouse was up and running smoothly now, and it was time to focus on other parts of our business back in our San Francisco office. Keith stayed behind in Kentucky to make sure things continued to run smoothly there. (He ended up living out of a hotel room in Kentucky for another two years before moving back to our headquarters.)

Our strategy of combining inventoried product with drop shipped product continued to drive our sales growth. We ended up doing $32 million in gross merchandise sales in 2002—almost four times what we had done in 2001.

The growth was exciting, but we also knew we were walking a tightrope. Our boost in sales had given us some additional runway before we ran out of cash. We were also able to talk to our vendors and convince some of them to allow us to take longer to pay them. We would have to figure out something over the next few months to solve our cash situation, but we knew we were on the right path.

Internally, we set an audacious long-term goal for Zappos: $1 billion in gross merchandise sales by 2010. It was a big number, but based on our growth rate so far, we felt confident that we could get there.

We just needed to make sure we didn't run out of cash over the next few months. Everyone could feel it: We were at a turning point for the company.

Whatever was going to happen over the next year would either make or break Zappos.

Growing Up

"What do we want to be when we grow up?"

It was a question I'd been thinking about for a while. I was at a Mexican restaurant with Fred, asking him the same question.

"Do we want to be about shoes, or do we want to be about something bigger?" I asked. "We can get to $1 billion in just footwear sales by 2010, but what about beyond that?"

"It would be pretty natural for us to expand into handbags and apparel," Fred said. "We could be the number one destination online for outfitting people from head to toe. We could appeal to every lifestyle—running, outdoors, fashion, and so on."

I thought back to my poker days and about the most important decision being which table to sit at. We had been sitting at the online footwear sales table. It was time to make a switch and move to a bigger table. I wondered if we could think of something even bigger than shoes, handbags, and apparel online.

"We had a customer e-mail us the other day," I said. "He had ordered a pair of shoes that we had in our warehouse and we surprised him with a shipping upgrade so that he got his order in two days instead of our original promise of a week. He said he loved our customer service and would tell his friends and family about us. He even said we should one day start a Zappos Airlines."

"That's pretty funny," Fred said.

"Have you read *Good to Great* by Jim Collins?" I asked.

"No, is it a good book? I mean ... is it a great book?"

"Yeah, you should definitely read it," I replied. "He talks about what separates the great companies from just the good ones over the long term. One of the things that he found from his research was that great companies have a greater purpose and bigger vision beyond just making money or being number one in a market. A lot of companies fall into the trap of just focusing on making money, and then they never become a great company."

"Well," Fred replied, "making money would certainly be a nice problem for us to have right now."

"We'll get there. We just need to get through this year. We had a good phone call with Wells Fargo today, so maybe we can get a loan from them."

"What are the chances of that happening?" Fred asked.

"It's too early to tell. But at least they didn't flat-out say no like all the other banks we tried to contact."

Fred and I continued talking. On the one hand, we had to get through our short-term cash-flow challenges. On the other hand, we wanted to make sure we were thinking long-term and laying the foundation for the future of the company. We knew we couldn't choose one over the other. We had to do both.

By the end of lunch, we realized that the biggest vision would be to build the Zappos brand to be about the very best customer service. Maybe one day there really would be a Zappos Airlines that would just be about the very best customer service and customer experience.

We talked about how the Zappos brand could be like the Virgin brand and be applied to many different types of businesses. The difference was that we thought the Virgin brand was more about being hip and cool, whereas we just wanted the Zappos brand to be about the very best customer service. Customer service had always been important at Zappos, but making it the focus of our brand would be a bold move, especially for an online company.

"Let's sleep on this for a while and see if we still feel good about it in a week or two," I said.

"Sounds good," Fred said. "You know, we could apply the whole service mentality to our vendors as well. That's never really been done before in the industry. We already treat our vendors well, but we can build up our reputation within the vendor community even more by really treating our vendors as true partners in the business. Most vendors aren't happy dealing with most retailers because the retailers, especially the department stores, usually try to squeeze every last dollar out of them. We could be the first major retailer that doesn't try to do that."

I nodded, thinking of the possibilities.

Fred looked at me. "By the way, do you have any other books you would recommend reading?"

"Yeah, there are a lot of really good business books out there. I'll give you a few of the ones that I really like."

Fred sent me an e-mail the next day.

> Date: February 17, 2003
> From: Fred Mossler
> To: Tony Hsieh
> Subject: Books
>   I was thinking about our book conversation. Maybe a cool way of encouraging people to read would be to create a board with everyone's names down one side and recommended books along the top. When a person completes one, they would get a check mark in the box. Perhaps, you would take to lunch once a month, the people that have completed the recommended books? Or maybe they would get movie tickets or gift certificates for completing three books, etc.
>   We could have a Zappos library with a couple copies of each of the books so people could check them out?

We didn't realize it at the time, but the idea of the Zappos library would evolve far beyond just a small set of books that a few employees would read. Five years later, there would be a hundred titles in our lobby available for free to all of our employees and visitors. Many of the books would eventually become required reading for our employees to help them pursue growth and learning, and Zappos would even offer classes to go over some of the more popular books.

A month later, we still weren't profitable. We still couldn't raise funding.

But we had a decision to make.

How serious were we about this idea of making the Zappos brand be about the very best customer service? We had discussed the idea internally with our employees, and everyone was excited about the potential new direction.

But was it all talk? Or were we committed?

We hadn't actually changed the way we did anything at Zappos yet. We did a lot of talking, but we weren't putting our money where our mouths were. And our employees knew it.

At the time, about 75 percent of our sales were coming from inventoried product. If it wasn't for our decision to start carrying inventory, our gross merchandise sales in 2002 would have been $8 million instead of $32 million.

For 2003, we were projecting sales to double, with about 25 percent of our overall sales coming from our drop ship business. The drop ship business was easy money. We didn't have to carry inventory so we didn't have any inventory risk or cash-flow problems with that part of the business. But we had plenty of customer service challenges.

The inventory feeds that we were getting from our vendors for our drop ship business were 95 percent accurate at best, meaning that we would not be able to actually fulfill 5 percent of all of our drop ship orders. On top of that, the brands did not ship as quickly or accurately as our own WHISKY warehouse, which meant we had plenty of unhappy and disappointed customers. But it was easy money.

We all knew deep down inside that we would have to give up the drop ship business sooner or later if we were serious about building the Zappos brand to be about the very best customer service. We also knew that the bigger we grew, the more reliant we would be on the cash from drop shipping. There would never be a good time to walk away. The longer we waited to pull the trigger, the more our employees would lose faith in us.

So we made what was both the easiest and hardest decision we ever had to make up until that point. In March 2003, with the flip of a switch, we turned off that part of our business and removed all of the drop ship products from our Web site.

We took a deep breath and hoped for the best. We knew in the back of our minds that there was a small chance we could get a loan from Wells Fargo, but we had only had phone conversations with them so far. Even if everything went smoothly, getting a loan was at least a few months away. We were truly testing our faith that we had made the right decision for the company.

We had to deal with our first test of our new direction right away. With the drop in revenue, cash was even tighter than before.

Now we had to figure out how to make next week's payroll.

Juggling Act

"Well," I said to Fred, "we can either pay our employees or pay all of our vendors. How do you think our vendors will feel if we pay them late?"

"It's definitely not ideal," he said, "but I guess we don't really have a choice. We'll just make sure that we're in constant communication with them, and try to get extended payment terms with as many of them as possible."

"Okay," I replied. "I'm going to e-mail you a spreadsheet of all the invoices that are due this week, and I need you to highlight the ones that we should pay first. This week, we have enough cash to pay about 70 percent of our vendors."

For the next several months, Fred and I repeated this routine every week. I left it up to Fred to decide which vendors to pay. Sometimes he chose vendors who had called the week before wondering when they were going to get paid, and other times he chose vendors we were most concerned about negatively impacting our relationships with. As Fred had said, it was definitely not ideal, but we felt like we really had no other choice.

In the background, conversations with Wells Fargo appeared to be going well. We were asking them to give us a $6 million line of credit. They hadn't given a loan to an unprofitable Internet company before, but the people that we were talking to could sense the passion we had for the business and were impressed with our growth rate. We found out later that internally at Wells Fargo there was a lot of debate as to whether they should stray outside of their norm and risk giving us a loan.

I think Fred and I felt the most stressed about the situation because we had a weekly reminder when we tried to figure out the best way to juggle our payables without hurting any of our vendor relationships. We felt that we were right on the tipping point of taking the company to the next level, but if the Wells Fargo loan didn't come through, then sooner or later our accounts payable situation would catch up to us and we'd be out of business. Our accounting and software development teams were scrambling trying to meet all of Wells Fargo's due diligence requests, providing them with the information they wanted as quickly as possible.

It was like being deep underwater, trying to swim up to the surface as quickly as possible to get a lifesaving gasp of oxygen. We could even see the surface from where we were. We were worried we would drown before we could come up for air, but we knew that if we made it, then we'd be home free. We were teetering right on the edge between death and a long healthy life ahead. There really was no in-between.

We really hoped that Wells Fargo would come through for us before our time was up.

*   *   *

And then, one day in June 2003, just as Fred and I were finishing up deciding which vendors to pay that week, we got the phone call from Wells Fargo. Everything had been approved on their end, and they were ready to sign the loan document.

Zappos was saved.

We signed the documents and breathed a collective sigh of relief. I think we all felt like we had lived through a scene from *Indiana Jones*, just narrowly escaping certain death by rolling under a falling stone door at the very last second while somehow still managing to keep our hats on.

We had done it. We had somehow survived. It still didn't seem real.

But it was.

I decided to write an e-mail to our employees, vendors, and friends of Zappos to spread the good news.

> Date: June 19, 2003
> From: Tony Hsieh
> To: Friends of Zappos
>
> For the past 2 months, we've been working with Wells Fargo on getting a revolving line of credit so that we can increase the amount of inventory in our warehouse. We finally closed the deal this morning, and I'm happy to announce that Zappos now has access to a line of credit of up to $6 million.
>
> For the first time in Zappos history, we now have over 200,000 pairs of shoes in our warehouse. While $6 million may seem like a lot, it is only when we combine it with the extended payment terms that we are getting with our top brands that will allow us to build out our warehouse and grow our inventory to a high enough level to support our rapid growth. The plan is to have over 600,000 pairs of shoes in our warehouse by the end of next year, so that we can offer a truly amazing selection for all of our customers.

For those of you who don't know, this month is the 4-year anniversary for Zappos. Here's a quick look at our sales over the past 4 years:

1999: Almost nothing

2000: $1.6 million

2001: $8.6 million

2002: $32 million

For 2003, we are on track to reach $60–$65 million in sales—double last year's sales numbers. This, however, is only the beginning. With getting our first line of credit from a bank, we've moved from the "building the runway" chapter of the company's life cycle to "getting ready for takeoff."

We are now enabled to really take the company to the next level, assuming we spend the money as carefully as we've been spending it up to this point. There are plenty of examples of companies with a lot more money that have gone out of business because they became careless or overconfident, celebrating their past successes instead of carefully navigating for the future.

If we spend our money carefully and continue to constantly improve the customer experience, we will reach over $1 billion in shoe sales a year in the not too distant future. I know $1 billion sounds impossible at first—but so did our current sales volume 3 years ago. But the reality is, it's actually not that crazy a number, and it's a very achievable goal: By 2010, total footwear sales in the US will be over $50 billion a year. Online footwear sales will be 10% of that—$5 billion a year. If we continue to be the leader in our space because of our relentless focus on improving the customer experience, then there is no reason why we won't be doing at least 20% of all online footwear sales by then. In fact, we have the potential to be doing a lot more.

Already, we've done a lot of revolutionary things that our customers love. We have the best in-stock shoe selection available anywhere, offline or online. We provide free shipping and free return shipping...for all of our customers as a standard part of our service. And although we promise our customers they will receive their shoes within 4–5 days, we upgrade the service for almost all of our customers....It's not something we have to do, and it's not something that will increase our profits in the short-term. But because it's something that creates a great customer experience, we choose to do it, because we believe that in the long run, little things that keep the customer in mind will end up paying huge dividends.

Our goal in doing all this is to one day become the #1 e-commerce company. We will out-Amazon Amazon in terms of being the most customer-centric online company. Although we happen to sell shoes today, we've built and will continue to build the platform for a great customer experience. This will allow us to one day expand into other categories beyond just shoes. But for now, it's important for us to remain focused on being the leader in online footwear sales, in terms of both selection and service.

I'd like to thank all of our employees, investors, vendors, and other partners for helping us get as far as we've gotten....

We've already been through a lot over the past 4 years, but the road ahead is as exciting as ever. There will be a lot of changes ahead as we grow, but one thing will always be constant: our focus on constantly improving the customer experience.

Tony Hsieh
CEO—Zappos.com

We paid off all of our overdue invoices later that week and had a happy hour to celebrate.

There was still a feeling of disbelief.

We no longer needed to worry about survival anymore. Now we could just focus on building something great for the long term.

We ended 2003 doing $70 million in gross merchandise sales, surpassing our own internal projections from just six months earlier. To reward everyone for their hard work, we decided to fly employees from San Francisco and Kentucky to Las Vegas for a weekend of celebration. Everyone had a great time. One of our employees ended up dancing next to Britney Spears the weekend she got married.

We were in Vegas as tourists, and the lights seemed magical and like a dream. Little did we know that less than a month later, we would decide to shut down our headquarters and move everybody from San Francisco to Las Vegas.

The next turning point for the company was right around the corner, and none of us had the foggiest idea that it was coming.

5

Platform for Growth: Brand, Culture, Pipeline

Viva Las Vegas

In San Francisco, we were having a hard time finding people who wanted to work in our customer service department. Even when we could hire good people, we discovered that most of them viewed customer service as a temporary job, something to bring in some extra money while they were going to school or separately pursuing their real career or calling.

Part of the problem was the high cost of living, and part of the problem was the culture. Working in a call center just wasn't something that people in the Bay Area wanted to do.

Toward the end of 2003, we started looking around at different options for expanding our call center. We initially considered outsourcing our call center overseas to India or the Philippines, but we remembered our hard lesson from working with eLogistics: *Never outsource your core competency.* If we were trying to build our brand to be about the very best customer service, we knew that we shouldn't be outsourcing that department.

Wherever we decided to open up our call center, we had to own and run it ourselves. After some research, we narrowed the list of possible locations down to Phoenix, Louisville, Portland, Des Moines, Sioux City, and Las Vegas.

Our original plan was simply to open up a satellite call center, but as we thought more about it, we realized that if we did that, our actions wouldn't really be matching our words. To build the Zappos brand into being about the very best customer service, we needed to make sure customer service was the entire company, not just a department. We needed to move our entire headquarters from San Francisco to wherever we wanted to build out our call center, which we had recently named our Customer Loyalty Team (or just CLT).

A few of us discussed this at lunch one day and thought about the different options we had. In the end, we decided that Las Vegas would be the best move for the company. It wasn't the cheapest option for us, but we thought it would make our existing employees the happiest.

Two days later, we held a company meeting and announced that we were relocating our headquarters to Las Vegas. We said that we would move our Customer Loyalty Team there first, with the goal of having everyone else in Vegas within six months.

When the announcement was made, everyone in the conference room was in a state of shock. We told everyone to take a week before making a decision one way or another. We had about ninety employees in San Francisco at the time, and I had thought maybe half of them would decide to uproot their lives and move with the company.

A week later, I was pleasantly surprised to learn that seventy employees were willing to give Vegas a shot and see what would happen. In their minds, it was all about being adventurous and open-minded. By that time, many of the Venture Frogs Incubator employees had become full-time Zappos employees and decided to move with Zappos as well.

Galen's Vegas Story

Five days prior to joining Zappos in San Francisco, I had officially become a married man. It was an exciting time and I was ready for the adventures life was about to bring. Or so I thought.

When I started work, HR told me Tony offered everybody a free membership to the gym that was located a couple floors above Zappos. So my daily routine consisted of showing up at the office around 6:00 or 7:00 AM, catching up on e-mail, then heading up to the gym with Fred at about 8:00.

One day, we were on the elliptical machines and Fred started barraging me with questions about Las Vegas. What's the town like? How are housing prices? He went on and on, but since he knew my parents lived there, I didn't think much of it.

A couple days later, Zappos announced they were moving the entire company to Vegas. It had been ten days since I joined, and I was faced with telling my wife of fifteen days we might have to move.

I was ready for adventure, but I didn't think it would come quite that quickly.

It was a bit of a wrench, but because of my parents, I knew Vegas wasn't just about gambling, the Strip, and strip clubs. After some deliberation, I could see us making the move and, thank God, my wife said yes.

Aki's Vegas Story

I've always been really fond of San Francisco and I love the Bay Area. So when we initially heard about the relocation to Las Vegas, it was hard. I think all of us were wrestling with the idea of leaving our friends and family behind, and thinking to ourselves, *Seriously, we're moving?*

But the company wasn't comprised of four or five people, or even ten or twenty. There were ninety of us, and we had already developed tight relationships and friendships by working (and playing) together.

I realized there was something unique about Zappos when I looked around and saw that all of my friends happened to be my co-workers too. So I decided to do it. And although very few of us had friends or relatives living in Vegas, once we moved, the family unit that we developed in San Francisco meant we all had automatic friends and family upon arrival.

Looking back, I remember thinking that it was really hard for all of us. But over the years, we've been able to develop new roots, and here we are, still together.

Maura's Vegas Story

I had been working at Zappos for about six months when they announced the move.

My first reaction: "Hell, no! I'm not moving to Las Vegas!"

But after the initial shock, we talked about what we really thought, and it turned out that a good number of people wanted to relocate. I started feeling different, and asked myself, "Why not?" I knew I loved the company *and* my job, so why not try it out? Worst-case scenario, I could always move back.

When I first saw our new building in Vegas, I thought there was no way we'd ever fill it. It was so much larger than our San Francisco office, it felt like there was nobody in it. Everything was still being built out and phones weren't even installed yet, so we communicated exclusively through e-mail. We had a lot of work to do.

Now, almost five years later, we occupy two buildings that are even larger than the original one. It's been exciting times and I guess the fact that I'm still living here speaks for itself!

Although it seems obvious in retrospect, probably the biggest benefit of moving to Vegas was that nobody had any friends outside of Zappos, so we were all sort of forced to hang out with each other outside the office. It was an exciting time. We were all beginning a new chapter of our lives together and forming a new social network. We worked together and hung out together during almost all of our waking hours.

In San Francisco, we had always said that culture was important to the company, mostly because we didn't want to make the same mistake that I had made back during my LinkExchange days, when the company culture went completely downhill.

Now that we were in Vegas with nobody else to lean on except each other, culture became our number one priority, even more important than customer service. We thought that if we got the culture right, then building our brand to be about the very best customer service would happen naturally on its own.

To keep our culture strong, we wanted to make sure that we only hired people who we would also enjoy hanging out with outside the office. As it turned out, many of the best ideas came about while having drinks at a local bar.

There was a group of about ten of us hanging out one night talking about how we could make sure that we continued to hire only people who would fit into the Zappos culture. There was a new hire in the group, so I asked each person to talk about the Zappos culture. We each gave our own interpretation.

When everyone was done, I felt that the new hire had gotten a pretty good idea of our culture.

"I wish we had recorded our past twenty minutes of conversation so that we could show it to all new hires," I said.

"Yeah," someone else said. "That would have been pretty cool."

"Or we could have transcribed it and given it as a handout to prospective employees," someone else chimed in.

"You know what?" I said. "We should just ask *all* of our employees to write a few paragraphs about what the Zappos culture means to them, and compile it all into a book."

And just like that, the idea for the Zappos Culture Book was born, and it's been a part of Zappos ever since. Every year, a new edition of the Zappos Culture Book is produced, which we give out to prospective employees, vendors, and even customers.

I sent the following e-mail to all of our employees in August 2004:

> From: Tony Hsieh
> To: All Zappos Employees
> Subject: Zappos Culture Book
>   We will be putting together a mini-book as part of the orientation package for all new hires about the Zappos culture. Our culture is the combination of all of our employees' ideas about the culture, so we would like to include everyone's thoughts in this book.
>   Please email me 100–500 words about what the Zappos culture means to you. (What is the Zappos culture? What's different about it compared to other company cultures? What do you like about our culture?)
>   We will compile everyone's contribution into the book. If you wish for your entry to be anonymous, please indicate so in your response. We will be distributing the book to all new hires as well as all existing employees.
>   Also, please do not talk to anyone about what you will be writing or what anyone else wrote. We want to know what the Zappos culture means to you specifically, as it will be different for different people.

We wanted to be as transparent as possible, so we decided that none of the entries would be censored or edited, except for typos. Every edition of our culture book includes both the good and the bad so that people reading the book can get a real sense of what our culture is like. With each new edition, it would also be a way of documenting how our culture was evolving over time.

While the vast majority of the entries in our first culture book were positive, we also learned that not every employee was thrilled about the company's growth. A couple of early Zappos employees complained about the additional processes and procedures that we had implemented and not being able to do things the way we used to. Some things, like filling out expense reports, were necessary by-products of our growth. Other things, such as criticism about communication within the company being harder than before, served as a wake-up call for us to be more proactive on that front.

Ask Anything

The feedback from the culture book led us to launch a monthly employee newsletter called *Ask Anything,* which is literally just that: Employees are encouraged to send an e-mail and ask any question they want. The anonymous questions and answers are compiled each month and e-mailed to the entire company. We continue to receive great questions from our employees. A sample of some of the questions that have been asked:

- When is the holiday party?
- Who is on the Zappos.com board of directors?
- What other music have we considered having as our hold music?
- I have heard that there are some brands being discontinued. Do you know which brands are being discontinued?
- Where do you see us in 3 years? How big, how many, and where?
- Why are women's and men's shoe sizes different?
- How many people at Zappos.com have the same birthday and anniversary date? Any one day more than others?
- What's the most expensive item we have ever had on our site?
- How much does Zappos spend on shipping (to and from) in any given month?
- Do vegetarians eat animal crackers?

We spent the next several years focusing on improving the customer experience, strengthening our culture, and investing in our employees' personal and professional development.

Our sales continued to grow, driven primarily by repeat customers and word of mouth. Eventually, Sequoia ended up investing in Zappos, Alfred moved to Vegas and joined the company full-time as CFO, we built out our board of directors, and Wells Fargo in conjunction with two other banks increased our credit line over time to $100 million.

It felt strange to have gone from the brink of going out of business to such rapid growth over such a short period of time. We didn't know it at the time, but all the hard work and investments we made into customer service and company culture would pave the way for us to hit our goal of $1 billion in gross merchandise sales in 2008—two years ahead of our original goal of 2010.

Looking back, a big reason we hit our goal early was that we decided to invest our time, money, and resources into three key areas: customer service (which would build our brand and drive word of mouth), culture (which would lead to the formation of our core values), and employee training and development (which would eventually lead to the creation of our Pipeline Team).

Even today, our belief is that our Brand, our Culture, and our Pipeline (which we internally refer to as "BCP") are the only competitive advantages that we will have in the long run.

Everything else can and will eventually be copied.

Cultivating the Culture Book
by Jenn

If you had to describe your company's culture in two or three paragraphs, what would you say? If you asked your co-workers to do the same, how similar (or different) do you think their answers would be?

When Tony first talked to me about creating a culture book, my interest was piqued. It was such an unusual idea—one that no one had ever done in quite the same way. What Tony was contemplating was counterintuitive and somewhat risky.

At the young age of five, Zappos had just begun focusing its attention on brand and culture. The 10 Core Values weren't fully established yet, but a culture book seemed like a powerful way to focus the company on the core values—because all of the content would come from the source of those values, the people who worked at Zappos.

The original idea was simple. We would ask employees to write, in a few paragraphs, the answer to the question: *What does Zappos culture mean to you?* Except for correcting typos, we would leave it unedited and publish everything in a book.

Completely unedited? That's crazy!

A few seconds (and probably a vodka shot or two) later... *Yeah, let's do it!*

For Zappos, it was a risk worth taking. If the company was truly going to stand behind its culture and core values, there couldn't be a better way to see if Zappos was doing it right.

What began as an off the cuff idea five years ago has now become something bigger. It started as a medium where employees could freely express themselves, and a way everyone could get a pulse of where the company's culture and core values stood. Over time, we asked vendors, partners and customers to contribute their perspectives too.

Today, it's become a book of reference for anyone remotely interested in Zappos, be it as a job applicant, a small business owner, or a future entrepreneur. Above all, because the company believes culture is an essential part of its business, it has become the brand book.

Over the years, I've always seen Zappos put its money where it matters most (even when it was incredibly scary), and the Culture Book is a great example of that. I can't think of a company that both talked and walked the same line as consistently as Zappos, taking risks on ideas *before* they were proven, before it was a billion-dollar company.

In an age of transparency, when Twitter can contribute to a company's success or its downfall, is there anything more compelling than exposing your company's DNA to the world?

Because of this, people wonder whether creating a culture book makes sense for their organization. If you've thought about it too, here are a few things worth considering:

1. The Culture Book is not about the book...it's about the culture.

If someone asked you to recite your corporate values or mission statement without looking it up, could you? People wonder how Zappos employees somehow remember all 10 Core Values by heart. To me, it's simple...it's easy when your company's core values are ones that apply not just to work, but to *life*.

In the section about Core Values that follows (page 155), you'll read stories of how Zappos employees apply the same values outside the office. Without a separation of work and life, it's remarkable how values can be exactly the same.

Before you create a culture book of your own, ask yourself:

Would you be comfortable printing everything your employees, customers, and partners have to say about your culture?

If not, what would it take for you to get there?

No culture book is worth much unless it reflects culture and values that are already in place.

2. It's a short-term expense, long-term investment.

Once you have a culture—*invest* in it. To some companies, thinking long-term may be completely irrational. Spending money on printing and shipping a physical book in this technological age may sound wasteful and foolish. It's true, it's hard to calculate the ROI of each culture book printed. But when you're trying to build a sustainable brand and create customer loyalty, sometimes saving money is not the point. The return you get from passionate people vouching for your company and culture, and the word of mouth that generates, is going to be intangible at the beginning. But over time, as it did for Zappos, the investment will pay off manyfold.

3. Make it available to everyone.

We began by giving a copy to all the employees and partners who contributed to the book. Now the Culture Book is available to the general public (see the Appendix for more information). That always blows my mind—people are *asking* to read the Culture Book of someone else's company. When's the last time you've heard of anyone requesting to read a company's annual report or employee handbook (outside of an investor or someone in HR)? It's incredible to think people might not even know what Zappos sells, but they still want to know what's behind the idea of the Culture Book. Somewhere down the line, that person just might think of Zappos next time she or he needs a new pair of jeans or shoes. (And it's worth a mention that book production costs are much more reasonable than you'd think.)

4. Give your evangelists a voice.

This past year was the first time we asked Zappos customers to get involved in the process. The response was amazing. We received submissions from all over the world, as well as e-mails from people who wished they lived in Kentucky or Nevada so they could apply for a job. But in the meantime, they'd love to be in a book associated with a company like Zappos.

In the earlier years, we asked vendors and partners to be involved too. For a company that's relied heavily on word of mouth, it's become a valuable channel of communication. Not only is it educational to hear from them, it lets customers and partners know how important they are to Zappos too.

5. A word is a word, and a picture is worth a thousand...but a brand is worth a million.

How do you convey something as intangible as a brand in something called the Culture Book?

Short answer? If your culture stays true to its values and/or mission statement, the words and images speak for themselves. Why? Because they're real.

Every voice in the book is a unique perspective, but together, they're the gestalt of Zappos. Why does an employee on page 40 sound strangely similar to someone else on page 128 or 340? It's because everyone at Zappos lives by the 10 Core Values. By sharing a common belief system, Zappos employees become the unified brand to the world. (As an aside, I'm always amused by people who say, "Zappos must be a cult!" In some ways, it is. But if a cult revolves around making people happy, I'll sign up anytime.)

Then comes the pictures part. By sprinkling in images of what the Zappos family does from morning to night—Marshmallow Peeps® contests, happy hours, Zolidays, the annual vendor party—we give readers a true sense of the brand in a non-obtrusive way. These aren't ads—these are pictures from our lives.

6. Not all cultures are the same.

In all likelihood, your company's book will look nothing like the Zappos Culture Book. It's not because one's any better than the other, it's just because your values and mission are unique to your own company's thumbprint. Make it a true voice of what your culture represents and it'll sing like it's in the shower.

7. Evolve.

If you're still unsure of whether a culture book makes sense for your company, one way to get a pulse is to send out an e-mail (or survey) first, asking your employees, partners and customers (or a subset of them) what they think your company's culture means to them. Now more than ever, they'll tell you the truth.

We had no idea what the results would be when we did this, but the most educational part of the exercise was that we took it and evolved. Our original idea soon morphed into something more interesting. We welcomed negative feedback knowing we'd learn and see whether the culture "reads" the same or different from the year before. If it's not in closer alignment to a company's values, goals, or mission, there's no doubt you'll know.

Forty years from now, I imagine I'll be sitting on my rocking chair, browsing Zappos.com like I'm in *Minority Report,* tapping the air in front of me to pick out what I'm going to wear for my nephew's wedding. Who knows, maybe I'll be booking my flight on Zappos Airlines too. I'm not sure what form of the Culture Book will exist at that point, but I do know one thing...I'll be reminiscing about those early Zappos days with a smile.

Branding Through Customer Service

Over the years, the number one driver of our growth at Zappos has been repeat customers and word of mouth. Our philosophy has been to take most of the money we would have spent on paid advertising and invest it into customer service and the customer experience instead, letting our customers do the marketing for us through word of mouth.

So what is great customer service?

It starts with what customers first see when they visit our Web site. In the United States, we offer free shipping both ways to make the transaction as easy as possible and risk-free for our customers. A lot of customers will order five different pairs of shoes, try them on with five different outfits in the comfort of their living rooms, and then send back the ones that don't fit or they simply don't like—free of charge. The additional shipping costs are expensive for us, but we really view those costs as a marketing expense.

We also offer a 365-day return policy for people who have trouble committing or making up their minds.

At most Web sites, the contact information is usually buried at least five links deep and even when you find it, it's a form or e-mail address that you can only contact once. We take the exact opposite approach. We put our phone number (1-800-927-7671) at the top of every single page of our Web site, because we actually want to talk to our customers. And we staff our call center 24/7.

I personally think it's kind of funny when I attend marketing or branding conferences and hear companies talk about consumers being bombarded with thousands and thousands of advertising messages every day, because there's usually a lot of discussion among companies and ad agencies talking about how to get their message to stand out.

There's a lot of buzz these days about "social media" and "integration marketing." As unsexy and low-tech as it may sound, our belief is that the telephone is one of the best branding devices out there. You have the customer's undivided attention for five to ten minutes, and if you get the interaction right, what we've found is that the customer remembers the experience for a very long time and tells his or her friends about it.

Too many companies think of their call centers as an expense to minimize. We believe that it's a huge untapped opportunity for most companies, not only because it can result in word-of-mouth marketing, but because of its potential to increase the lifetime value of the customer.

Usually marketing departments assume that the lifetime value of a customer is fixed when doing their ROI calculations. We view the lifetime value of a customer to be a moving target that can increase if we can create more and more positive emotional associations with our brand through every interaction that a person has with us.

Another common trap that many marketers fall into is focusing too much on trying to figure out how to generate a lot of buzz, when really they should be focused on building engagement and trust.

I can tell you that my mom has zero buzz, but when she says something, I listen.

To that end, most of our efforts on the customer service and customer experience side actually happen *after* we've already made the sale and taken a customer's credit card number. For example, for most of our loyal repeat customers, we do surprise upgrades to overnight shipping, even though we only promise them standard ground shipping when they choose the free shipping option.

In conjunction with that, we run our warehouse 24/7, which actually isn't the most efficient way to run a warehouse. The most efficient way to run a warehouse is to let the orders pile up, so that when a warehouse worker needs to walk around the warehouse to pick the orders, the picking density is higher, so the picker has less of a distance to walk. But we're not trying to maximize for picking efficiency. We're trying to maximize the customer experience, which in the e-commerce business is defined in part by getting orders out to our customers as quickly as possible.

The combination of a 24/7 warehouse, surprise upgrades to overnight shipping, and having our warehouse located just fifteen minutes away from the UPS Worldport hub means that a lot of customers order as late as midnight EST, and are surprised when their orders show up on their doorstep eight hours later. This creates a WOW experience, which our customers remember for a very long time and tell their friends and family about.

We receive thousands and thousands of phone calls and e-mails every single day, and we really view each contact as an opportunity to build the Zappos brand into being about the very best customer service and customer experience. Seeing every interaction through a branding lens instead of an expense-minimization lens means we run our call center very differently from most call centers.

Most call centers measure their employees' performance based on what's known in the industry as "average handle time," which focuses on how many phone calls each rep can take in a day. This translates into reps worrying about how quickly they can get a customer off the phone, which in our eyes is not delivering great customer service. Most call centers also have scripts and force their reps to try to upsell customers to generate additional revenue.

At Zappos, we don't measure call times (our longest phone call was almost six hours long!), and we don't upsell. We just care about whether the rep goes above and beyond for every customer. We don't have scripts because we trust our employees to use their best judgment when dealing with each and every customer. We want our reps to let their true personalities shine during each phone call so that they can develop a personal emotional connection (internally referred to as PEC) with the customer.

Another example of us using the telephone as a branding device is what happens when a customer calls looking for a specific style of shoes in a specific size that we're out of stock on. In those instances, every rep is trained to research at least three competitors' Web sites, and if the shoe is found in stock to direct the customer to the competitor. Obviously, in those situations, we lose the sale. But we're not trying to maximize each and every transaction. Instead, we're trying to build a lifelong relationship with each customer, one phone call at a time.

A lot of people may think it's strange that an Internet company is so focused on the telephone, when only about 5 percent of our sales happen through the telephone. In fact, most of our phone calls don't even result in sales. But what we've found is that on average, every customer contacts us at least once sometime during his or her lifetime, and we just need to make sure that we use that opportunity to create a lasting memory.

The majority of phone calls don't result in an immediate order.

Sometimes a customer may be calling because it's her first time returning an item, and she just wants a little help stepping through the process. Other times, a customer may call because there's a wedding coming up this weekend and he wants a little fashion advice. And sometimes, we get customers who call simply because they're a little lonely and want someone to talk to.

I'm reminded of a time when I was in Santa Monica, California, a few years ago at a Skechers sales conference. After a long night of bar-hopping, a small group of us headed up to someone's hotel room to order some food. My friend from Skechers tried to order a pepperoni pizza from the room-service menu, but was disappointed to learn that the hotel we were staying at did not deliver hot food after 11:00 PM. We had missed the deadline by several hours.

In our inebriated state, a few of us cajoled her into calling Zappos to try to order a pizza. She took us up on our dare, turned on the speakerphone, and explained to the (very) patient Zappos rep that she was staying in a Santa Monica hotel and really craving a pepperoni pizza, that room service was no longer delivering hot food, and that she wanted to know if there was anything Zappos could do to help.

The Zappos rep was initially a bit confused by the request, but she quickly recovered and put us on hold. She returned two minutes later, listing the five closest places in the Santa Monica area that were still open and delivering pizzas at that time.

Now, truth be told, I was a little hesitant to include this story because I don't actually want everyone who reads this book to start calling Zappos and ordering pizza. But I just think it's a fun story to illustrate the power of *not* having scripts in your call center and empowering your employees to do what's right for your brand, no matter how unusual or bizarre the situation.

As for my friend from Skechers? After that phone call, she's now a customer for life.

Top 10 Ways to Instill Customer Service into Your Company

1. Make customer service a priority for the whole company, not just a department. A customer service attitude needs to come from the top.
2. Make *WOW* a verb that is part of your company's everyday vocabulary.
3. Empower and trust your customer service reps. Trust that they want to provide great service…because they actually do. Escalations to a supervisor should be rare.
4. Realize that it's okay to fire customers who are insatiable or abuse your employees.
5. Don't measure call times, don't force employees to upsell, and don't use scripts.
6. Don't hide your 1-800 number. It's a message not just to your customers, but to your employees as well.
7. View each call as an investment in building a customer service brand, not as an expense you're seeking to minimize.
8. Have the entire company celebrate great service. Tell stories of WOW experiences to everyone in the company.
9. Find and hire people who are already passionate about customer service.
10. Give great service to everyone: customers, employees, and vendors.

Culture

Today, we offer tours of our headquarters in Las Vegas to the general public. Tours take about an hour, and we open ourselves up to the public because we've found that it's a great way for people to get a true sense of our culture. It's one thing to read about it, but almost everyone who has gone on our tour tells us that it isn't until they actually visit our offices and *feel* our culture that they finally understand why it is so important.

It wasn't always this way. We certainly never planned to give public tours. It's just another example of something that evolved organically over time for us, and our employees chose to embrace it and take it to the next level.

Today, we work with more than a thousand different vendors. In the beginning, whenever a new vendor visited our offices, someone from our merchandising team would give them a tour of our operations. Over time, as word of mouth spread, we found that friends of our vendors wanted to get a tour, and eventually we started getting random requests from friends and customers to go on a tour.

In the early days, a tour would take less than ten minutes, but as more and more people started touring our offices, different groups within Zappos started to come up with different ideas on how to make each tour more and more of a WOW experience for our visitors.

Every tour is different, because you never know who is going to be in the office or what a team decided to do over the weekend to surprise our visitors. If you were to show up for a tour today, you might find a popcorn machine or a coffee machine dressed up as a robot in our lobby. As you passed through different departments, you might find an aisle of cowbells ("more cowbell?"), a make-shift bowling alley built by our software developers, employees dressed up as pirates, employees karaokeing, a nap room, a petting zoo, or a hot dog social. You might see a parade pass by because one of our departments decided that it was the perfect day to celebrate Oktoberfest. And you might say hi to our life coach (our own internal version of Tony Robbins), wear a crown, and get your picture taken and put up next to the pictures of Serena Williams or Gladys Knight when they came and toured our offices. Or you might happen to show up during our annual "Bald & Blue" day, where employees volunteer to get their heads shaved by other employees.

The Origins of Bald & Blue Day

Our annual Bald & Blue tradition started as a dare while a few of us were hanging out at a bar. An e-mail went out the next day.

Date: June 7, 2005
From: Renee N.
To: Las Vegas Zappos Employees
Subject: Bald is BEAUTIFUL
    Hello All,
    A challenge or should I say invitation (by someone who will remain nameless) has been put out to all the BRAVE men at Zappos to shave their heads BALD or shaved down to a number 1. Tony will be participating in shaving his head as well. We are looking for at least 30 men or more to take part in this "just because" event. So far we have 15 Brave Men.
    We need some women volunteers to help shave these brave men's heads and volunteers to bring in at least 5 clippers with the number 1 attachment. For those of us not participating in shaving our heads, please show your support by wearing your Zappos t-shirt and/or wearing your Zappos hats.
    This will take place tomorrow June 8th at 12:30 PM at the patio outside the lunchroom. Please respond to me ASAP if you'd like to participate in shaving your head or if you'd like to be a volunteer.
    Thanks!

Our employees know that our number one priority at Zappos is our company culture. While all of the things I just mentioned have come about organically (most of them I don't even know about until they've already happened), a few of the things we do are more purposeful and planned.

For example, we have all of our employees walk through a central reception area to get in and out of the building even though there are more convenient doors located closer to the parking lot. The previous tenants had used all the doors in our building for exiting, but we decided to mark all of them for use as emergency exits only. We made this decision when we moved into our building as part of our goal to build more of a community by increasing the chances of serendipitous employee interactions.

In most companies, logging in to the computer systems requires a login and password. At Zappos, an additional step is required: a photo of a randomly selected employee is displayed, and the user is given a multiple-choice test to name that employee. Afterward, the profile and bio of that employee are shown, so that everyone can learn more about each other. Although there is no penalty for giving the wrong answer, we do keep a record of everyone's score. Internally, we refer to this as "The Face Game."

We also try to measure the strength of our culture through regular employee surveys by asking employees whether they agree or disagree with statements such as:

- I believe that the company has a higher purpose beyond just profits.
- My role at Zappos has a real purpose—it is more than just a job.
- I feel that I am in control of my career path and that I am progressing in my personal and professional development at Zappos.
- I consider my co-workers to be like my family and friends.
- I am very happy in my job.

We're always on the lookout for ways to improve our company culture, no matter how unconventional or counterintuitive the approach may be. For example, a research study showed that "letting workers swear at will in the workplace can benefit employees and employers." The article went on to cite that "employees use swearing on a continuous basis, but not necessarily in a negative, abusive manner. Swearing is used as a social phenomenon to reflect solidarity and enhance group cohesiveness, or as a psychological phenomenon to release stress." We forwarded the article to our managers.

Over time, as we focused more and more on our culture, we ultimately came to the realization that a company's culture and a company's brand are really just two sides of the same coin. The brand is just a lagging indicator of a company's culture. This realization eventually led me to write the following blog post:

Your Culture Is Your Brand

Building a brand today is very different from building a brand 50 years ago. It used to be that a few people got together in a room, decided what the brand positioning was going to be, and then spent a lot of money buying advertising telling people what their brand was. And if you were able to spend enough money, then you were able to build your brand.

It's a very different world today. With the Internet connecting everyone together, companies are becoming more and more transparent whether they like it or not. An unhappy customer or a disgruntled employee can blog about a bad experience with a company, and the story can spread like wildfire by e-mail or with tools like Twitter.

The good news is that the reverse is true as well. A great experience with a company can be read by millions of people almost instantaneously as well.

The fundamental problem is that you can't possibly anticipate every possible touch point that could influence the perception of your company's brand.

For example, if you happen to meet an employee of Company X at a bar, even if the employee isn't working, how you perceive your interaction with that employee will affect how you perceive Company X, and therefore Company X's brand. It can be a positive influence, or a negative influence. Every employee can affect your company's brand, not just the front-line employees that are paid to talk to your customers.

At Zappos.com, we decided a long time ago that we didn't want our brand to be just about shoes, or clothing, or even online retailing. We decided that we wanted to build our brand to be about the very best customer service and the very best customer experience. We believe that customer service shouldn't be just a department, it should be the entire company.

Advertising can only get your brand so far. If you ask most people what the "brand" of the airline industry as a whole is (not any specific airline, but the entire industry), they will usually say something about bad customer service or bad customer experience. If you ask people what their perception of the US auto industry is today, chances are the responses you get won't be in line with what the automakers project in their advertising.

So what's a company to do if you can't just buy your way into building the brand you want?

What's the best way to build a brand for the long term?

In a word: culture.

At Zappos, our belief is that if you get the culture right, most of the other stuff—like great customer service, or building a great long-term brand, or passionate employees and customers—will happen naturally on its own.

We believe that your company's culture and your company's brand are really just two sides of the same coin. The brand may lag the culture at first, but eventually it will catch up.

Your culture is your brand.

So how do you build and maintain the culture that you want?

It starts with the hiring process. At Zappos, we actually do two different sets of interviews. The hiring manager and his/her team will do the standard set of interviews looking for relevant experience, technical ability, fit within the team, etc. But then our HR department does a separate set of interviews, looking purely for culture fit. Candidates have to pass both sets of interviews in order to be hired.

We've actually said no to a lot of very talented people that we know can make an immediate impact on our top or bottom line. But because we felt they weren't culture fits, we were willing to sacrifice the short-term benefits in order to protect our culture (and therefore our brand) for the long term.

After hiring, the next step to building the culture is training. Everyone that is hired into our headquarters goes through the same training that our Customer Loyalty Team (call center) reps go through, regardless of department or title. You might be an accountant, or a lawyer, or a software developer—you go through the exact same training program.

It's a 4-week training program, in which we go over company history, the importance of customer service, the long-term vision of the company, our philosophy about company culture— and then you're actually on the phone for 2 weeks, taking calls from customers. Again, this goes back to our belief that customer service shouldn't just be a department, it should be the entire company.

At the end of the first week of training, we make an offer to the entire class. We offer everyone $2,000 to quit (in addition to paying them for the time they've already worked), and it's a standing offer until the end of the fourth week of training. We want to make sure that employees are here for more than just a paycheck. We want employees that believe in our long-term vision and want to be a part of our culture. As it turns out, on average, less than 1% of people end up taking the offer.

One of the great advantages of focusing on culture is when reporters come and visit our offices. Unlike most companies, we don't give reporters a small list of people they're allowed to talk to. Instead, we encourage them to wander around and talk to whoever they want. It's our way of being as transparent as possible, which is part of our culture.

We've formally defined the Zappos culture in terms of 10 core values:

1. Deliver WOW Through Service
2. Embrace and Drive Change
3. Create Fun and a Little Weirdness
4. Be Adventurous, Creative, and Open-Minded
5. Pursue Growth and Learning
6. Build Open and Honest Relationships with Communication
7. Build a Positive Team and Family Spirit
8. Do More with Less
9. Be Passionate and Determined
10. Be Humble

Many companies have core values, but they don't really commit to them. They usually sound more like something you'd read in a press release. Maybe you learn about them on day 1 of orientation, but after that it's just a meaningless plaque on the wall of the lobby.

We believe that it's really important to come up with core values that you can commit to. And by commit, we mean that you're willing to hire and fire based on them. If you're willing to do that, then you're well on your way to building a company culture that is in line with the brand you want to build. You can let all of your employees be your brand ambassadors, not just the marketing or PR department. And they can be brand ambassadors both inside and outside the office.

At the end of the day, just remember that if you get the culture right, most of the other stuff—including building a great brand—will fall into place on its own.

Even though our core values guide us in everything we do today, we didn't actually have any formal core values for the first six or seven years of the company's history. It's my fault that we didn't do it in the early years, because it was something I'd always thought of as a very "corporate" thing to do. I resisted doing it for as long as possible.

I'm just glad that an employee finally convinced me that it was necessary to come up with core values—essentially, a formalized definition of our culture—in order for us to continue to scale and grow.

I only wish we had done it sooner.

Core Values

Back in San Francisco, Nick, Fred, and I tried to interview every prospective employee to make sure they were a culture fit for Zappos. When we moved the company to Vegas, we were hiring a lot of people very quickly due to our rapid growth. It wasn't scalable for us to be involved with every new hire decision, but the problem was that because we had so many new employees, not everyone knew exactly what we were looking for when we said we were looking for a culture fit.

Someone from our legal department suggested that we come up with a list of core values to serve as a guide for managers to make hiring decisions, so I started jotting down the things that we were looking for. I thought about all the employees I wanted to clone because they represented the Zappos culture well, and tried to figure out what values they personified. I also thought about all the employees and ex-employees who were not culture fits, and tried to figure out where there was a values disconnect.

As I started creating the list, I realized that I needed to get everyone's input on what our core values should be, just like we had done with the Culture Book, when we asked every employee for their thoughts on what the Zappos culture was.

The initial list had thirty-seven core values:

1) Culture Is Everything
2) WOW/Service

3) Trust and Faith
4) Idealism
5) Company Growth
6) Long Term
7) Personal Growth and Stretching
8) Achieving the Impossible
9) Team
10) Family/Relationships
11) Emotional Connections
12) Developing Your Gut
13) Empowerment
14) Ownership
15) Taking Initiative
16) Doing Whatever It Takes
17) Not Being Afraid to Make Mistakes
18) Unconventional
19) Bottom Up (Meets Top Down)
20) Partnerships
21) Listening
22) Overcommunicate
23) Operational Excellence
24) Built for Change
25) Continuous Incremental Improvement
26) Doing More with Less
27) Innovation
28) Word of Mouth
29) Lucky
30) Passion and Positivity
31) Personality
32) Openness and Honesty
33) Fun
34) Inspirational
35) A Little Weird

36) Willing to Laugh at Ourselves
37) Quiet Confidence and Respect

It was a long list, so we started thinking about which values were the most important and truly represented who we wanted to be. We also thought about whether we could combine some of them into a single core value.

Over the course of a year, I e-mailed the entire company several times and got a lot of suggestions and feedback on which core values were the most important to our employees.

I was surprised the process took so long, but we wanted to make sure not to rush through the process because whatever core values we eventually came up with, we wanted to be ones that we could truly embrace.

The commitment part was the most challenging part. As I mentioned in my "Your Culture Is Your Brand" blog post, a lot of corporations have "core values" or "guiding principles," but the problem is that they're usually very lofty sounding and they read like a press release that the marketing department put out. A lot of times, an employee might learn about them on day 1 of orientation, but then the values just end up being part of a meaningless plaque on the wall of the corporate lobby.

We wanted to make sure that didn't happen with our core values. We wanted a list of committable core values that we were willing to hire and fire on. If we weren't willing to do that, then they weren't really "values."

We eventually came up with our final list of ten core values, which we still use today:

1) Deliver WOW Through Service
2) Embrace and Drive Change
3) Create Fun and a Little Weirdness
4) Be Adventurous, Creative, and Open-Minded

5) Pursue Growth and Learning
6) Build Open and Honest Relationships with Communication
7) Build a Positive Team and Family Spirit
8) Do More with Less
9) Be Passionate and Determined
10) Be Humble

Integrity was a value that had been suggested by some employees, but I made a conscious choice to leave it out. I felt that integrity would come from us actually committing to and living up to our core values in everything we did, not just referring to them when it was convenient.

Over time, our recruiting department developed interview questions for each and every one of the core values, and we tested our commitment during the hiring process.

Be Humble is probably the core value that ends up affecting our hiring decisions the most. There are a lot of experienced, smart, and talented people we interview that we know can make an immediate impact on our top or bottom line. But a lot of them are also really egotistical, so we end up not hiring them. At most companies, the hiring manager would probably argue that we should hire such a candidate because he or she will add a lot of value to the company, which is probably why most large corporations don't have great cultures.

Our philosophy at Zappos is that we're willing to make short-term sacrifices (including lost revenue or profits) if we believe that the long-term benefits are worth it. Protecting the company culture and sticking to core values is a long-term benefit.

Once we had our final list of our ten core values, I sent an e-mail to the entire company describing each of them in more detail. We still refer to the original e-mail today. In fact, when new employees join the company, they are required to sign a document stating that they have read the core values document and understand that living up to the core values is part of their job expectation.

Zappos Core Values Document

THE ZAPPOS MISSION: To live and deliver WOW.

As we grow as a company, it has become more and more important to explicitly define the Zappos core values from which we develop our culture, our brand, and our business strategies. With so many new employees joining the company as we grow, we want to make sure that everyone is on the same page and acting consistently with what we want Zappos to be all about.

Over time, we will be restructuring performance evaluations so that a big part of every employee's performance evaluation is based on how well he/she represents and makes decisions based on the Zappos core values.

While there are many subcomponents to each value, we've distilled the most important themes into the following 10 core values.

1) Deliver WOW Through Service
2) Embrace and Drive Change
3) Create Fun and a Little Weirdness
4) Be Adventurous, Creative, and Open-Minded
5) Pursue Growth and Learning
6) Build Open and Honest Relationships with Communication
7) Build a Positive Team and Family Spirit
8) Do More with Less
9) Be Passionate and Determined
10) Be Humble

Ideally, we want all 10 core values to be reflected in everything we do, including how we interact with each other, how we interact with our customers, and how we interact with our vendors and business partners.

There is a lot of work that lies ahead, and it will be quite some time before our 10 core values are truly reflected in how we think, how we act, and how we communicate.

As we grow, our processes and strategies may change, but we want our values to always remain the same. Our core values should always be the framework from which we make all of our decisions. Because this is our first time publishing our core values, there may be some additions or changes made over the next year, but our goal is to ultimately decide on a final list of core values to serve as the framework for how we run and grow the company.

I encourage everyone to re-examine everything that is being done at the company and ask yourself what changes can be made to better reflect our core values. For example, our employee handbook could be improved so it sounds more like "Zappos" and less like an employee handbook that you might find at another company. The forms that we use internally, our job application forms, some of our e-mail templates, parts of our Web site, and much, much more can all be improved to feel more like Zappos and better reflect our core values.

So the challenge to everyone is this: Make at least one improvement every week that makes Zappos better reflect our core values.

The improvements don't have to be dramatic—it can be as simple as adding in an extra sentence or two to a form to make it more fun, for example. But if every employee made just one small improvement every week to better reflect our core values, then by the end of this year we will have over 50,000 small changes that collectively will be a very dramatic improvement compared to where we are today.

A brief description of each of the 10 core values is below.

Deliver WOW Through Service

At Zappos, anything worth doing is worth doing with WOW.

WOW is such a short, simple word, but it really encompasses a lot of things. To WOW, you must differentiate yourself, which means do something a little unconventional and innovative. You must do something that's above and beyond what's expected. And whatever you do must have an emotional impact on the receiver. We are not an average company, our service is not average, and we don't want our people to be average. We expect every employee to deliver WOW.

Whether internally with co-workers or externally with our customers and partners, delivering WOW results in word of mouth. Our philosophy at Zappos is to WOW with service and experience, not with anything that relates directly to monetary compensation (for example, we don't offer blanket discounts or promotions to customers).

We seek to WOW our customers, our co-workers, our vendors, our partners, and in the long run, our investors.

Ask yourself: What are things you can improve upon in your work or attitude to WOW more people? Have you WOWed at least one person today?

Deliver WOW Through Service
by Martha C.

In 1984, I had spent seven weeks traveling throughout Europe. By the time I got to London, my last stop before returning to the States, I had no money left except for my lucky US dollar and a handful of foreign coins at the bottom of my handbag.

Thirsty, I grabbed a soda from the snack bar and read the sign: FOREIGN MONEY ACCEPTED. By the time I reached the front of the register line, I had almost downed the whole can when I spotted another sign: NO FOREIGN COINS. PAPER CURRENCY ONLY. My attempt to convince the cashier to take all my coins was futile and the last thing I wanted to do was part with my lucky dollar.

Suddenly, the gentleman behind me reached over and paid for my soda. I thanked him and tried giving him all my coins but he refused. He just asked that I start doing random acts of kindness for others. That one incident with a stranger in the London airport stayed with me forever.

Fast-forwarding to last Tuesday morning, 2008, I just finished checking off my long shopping list at Walgreens and stepped up to the register. Two people who only had a few items got in line behind me so naturally I let them go first. When it was my turn, the cashier was about a third of the way through my items when an older gentleman filed in line. Two cans of peanuts, salve, and Chapstick were in his hands.

I turned to him and asked him to give them to me. With a puzzled look on his face, he asked why. I had completely meant to say, *It's a random act of kindness,* but instead the words "It's a random act of WOWness" came out of my mouth. Since working at Zappos, the word *WOW* replaced *kind* on its own. Rather than correct what I said, I just went with it. The cashier scanned and placed the items in a bag and handed it to the gentleman.

He looked at me and said, "Tell me about this 'random act of WOWness.'" He listened to my story about the stranger in London, profusely thanked me, and left the store. Now it was the cashier's turn to look at me strangely. He too wanted to know about "random acts of WOWness" and I explained how I work at Zappos and one of our core values is to WOW our customers.

Leaving that store, I had an incredible feeling. Not only did I share WOWness, I shared it with two people and could only hope they might pay it forward as well someday.

A few days later, on my way home from Zappos after my night shift, I walked in to the same Walgreens at 7:00 AM. I had barely stepped foot into the store when I heard, "Hi Martha." I realized it was the same cashier from the other day.

Surprised, I said, "I can't believe you remember my name." He replied, "I wrote your name down from the credit card receipt, because I didn't want to forget the person that taught me about 'random acts of WOW and kindness.' I've told others about it too!"

The funny thing was, he was the one now WOWing me in return.

Embrace and Drive Change

Part of being in a growing company is that change is constant. For some people, especially those who come from bigger companies, the constant change can be somewhat unsettling at first. If you are not prepared to deal with constant change, then you probably are not a good fit for the company.

We must all learn not only to not fear change, but to embrace it enthusiastically and, perhaps even more important, encourage and drive it. We must always plan for and be prepared for constant change.

Although change can and will come from all directions, it's important that most of the changes in the company are driven from the bottom up—from the people who are on the front lines, closer to the customers and/or issues.

Never accept or be too comfortable with the status quo, because the companies that get into trouble are historically the ones that aren't able to adapt to change and respond quickly enough.

We are ever evolving. If we want to continue to stay ahead of our competition, we must continually change and keep them guessing. Others can copy our images, our shipping, and the overall look of our Web site, but they cannot copy our people, our culture, or our service. And they will not be able to evolve as fast as we can as long as embracing constant change is part of our culture.

Ask yourself: How do you plan and prepare for change? Do you view new challenges optimistically? Do you encourage and drive change? How do you encourage more change to be driven from the bottom up?

Are you empowering your direct reports to drive change?

The Power of 1%
Blog post by Alfred L, CFO/COO, January 2009

It was the best of times and it was the worst of times.
—A Tale of Two Cities, *by Charles Dickens*

On *CNBC Reports* 2008, Maria Bartiromo quoted Charles Dickens, noting that, while Dickens was referring to the French Revolution, he could have easily been talking about 2008.

No doubt, 2008 was a very challenging year, starting out with a weak economic and retail environment that degraded slowly in the first half of the year and then fell off a cliff in the second half of the year. Depending on what reports you read, online e-commerce was down 3–5% this holiday season, marking the first time e-commerce didn't grow. Reading about these not-so-positive reports just goes to show how very lucky we are at Zappos, because we were able to ride through these rocky times and produce pretty incredible results.

No, things weren't perfect, but 2008 was still a great year for us! Official results have to wait until our finance team closes the books and releases the audited financials in early March, but we managed to grow our business over last year and during the holiday season (when e-commerce was down), exceeded $1B in gross merchandise sales. And by Doing More With Less, we kept ourselves profitable and cash-positive, all the while having a lot of fun serving our customers!

We can reminisce about 2008, but now that 2009 is here and we're back from some much-needed downtime, it's time to get our A-game back on. We'll be going over our goals and "official" plans as soon as our board approves them, but even before that "officially" happens, we already know what we need to do.

One thing I encourage you to do is to refer back to our core values document and make at least one improvement every week that makes Zappos better. Ideally, we would do this every single day. It sounds daunting, but remember improvements don't have to be dramatic. Think about what it means to improve just 1% per day and build upon that every single day. Doing so has a dramatic effect and will make us 37x better, not 365% (3.65x) better, at the end of the year.

Wake up every day and ask yourself not only what is the 1% improvement I can change to make Zappos better, but also what is the 1% improvement I can change to make *myself* better personally and professionally. In the end we, as Zappos, can't grow unless we, as individuals, grow too.

Imagine yourself making 1% changes every day that compound and consequently make you and Zappos 37x better by the end of the year. Imagine if every employee at Zappos was to do the same. Imagine how much better you, Zappos, and the world will be next year.

It won't be easy and 2009 will no doubt present its own set of challenges, but we positively will get through it. Have a great and happy 2009!

PS: This is for the math geeks. If you start out with $100 at the beginning of the year and you were able to increase what you have by 1% every single day, at the end of the year, you would have $3,778.34 = $100 * (1 + 1%) ^ 365. That is 37.78x what you had at the beginning of the year. Get that 1% every single day!

PPS: Yes, I am a math geek. No, I wasn't cool enough to join the football team, so I joined the math team. Thanks for putting up with me.

Create Fun and a Little Weirdness

One of the things that makes Zappos different from a lot of other companies is that we value being fun and being a little weird. We don't want to become one of those big companies that feel corporate and boring. We want to be able to laugh at ourselves. We look for both fun and humor in our daily work.

This means that many things we do might be a little unconventional—or else it wouldn't be a little weird. We're not looking for crazy or extreme weirdness though. We want just a touch of weirdness to make life more interesting and fun for everyone. We want the company to have a unique and memorable personality.

Our company culture is what makes us successful, and in our culture we celebrate and embrace our diversity and each person's individuality. We want people to express their personality in their work. To outsiders, that might come across as inconsistent or weird. But the consistency is in our belief that we function best when we can be ourselves. We want the weirdness in each of us to be expressed in our interactions with each other and in our work.

One of the side effects of encouraging weirdness is that it encourages people to think outside the box and be more innovative. When you combine a little weirdness with making sure everyone is also having fun at work, it ends up being a win–win for everyone: Employees are more engaged in the work that they do, and the company as a whole becomes more innovative.

Ask yourself: What can we do to be a little weird and differentiate ourselves from everyone else? What can we do that's both fun and a little weird? How much fun do you have in your job, and what can you do to make it more fun? What do you do to make your co-workers' jobs fun as well?

Fun and a Little Weird: Live Chat
A blog post by Todd, a Zappos customer

The reason I was testing out Zappos live chat was because I am "Cruiser in Chief" of a beach cruiser store, and I was curious how Zappos would handle my chat. Zappos is known for service… and for letting their service agents "be themselves." I put this to the test tonight and threw a curveball or two at the guy helping me in a live chat. I used the name "Timmy" as my alias and asked a totally random question about a random product. See actual chat log below. Zappos rocks! I could not even make this stuff up, I swear.

You are now chatting with Jonathan.

Jonathan: Hello Timmy. How can I help you?

Timmy: Do you know how wide the G-Shock Atomic Solar—AWG101 SKU #7403774 is?

Timmy: I mean, how big a wrist it would fit?

Timmy: Timmy has a big fat wrist

Timmy: Timmy need watch grande

Jonathan: I'll see what I can find out for Timmy.

Timmy: Awesome. And can we please continue to talk about Timmy in the 3rd person? Timmy likes to boost Timmy's ego by talking about Timmy that way

Jonathan: Jonathan would be happy to neglect the use of pronouns for the duration of this conversation.

Timmy: Jonathan and Timmy shall get along just fine

Jonathan: Will Timmy be able to measure Timmy's wrist?

Timmy: Timmy's wrist is big, but not Biggie-Smalls big. Timmy doesn't have the required measurement instruments.

Timmy: Timmy is 6'4" 220lbs if that helps Jonathan

Jonathan: Luckily, that is roughly the size of Jonathan's brother, so that does help.

Jonathan: Jonathan thinks that this watch will work out well for Timmy. The watch's circumference is 9 inches, so it will probably fit around Timmy's wrist.

Timmy: Ok cool

Timmy: Do your watches and stuff have free return shipping like your Zapatos?

Timmy: In case Timmy wants another one or something

Jonathan: And if it doesn't work out, as long as the watch is in its original condition and in the original packaging, Timmy has 365 days to return Timmy's order. We will even pay for the return shipping! As always, our shipping to Timmy will be free.

Timmy: Timmy thanks Jonathan for good help

Jonathan: Jonathan welcomes Timmy.

Jonathan: It's Jonathan's pleasure!

Jonathan: Can Jonathan do anything more for Timmy?

Timmy: No that is all Timmy needs

Timmy: Timmy happy

Jonathan: Good. Does Timmy have an account set up with Zappos yet?

Jonathan: Jonathan will upgrade Timmy's account.

Timmy: Yes Timmy is repeat shopper

Timmy: But "Timmy" is my alter ego and not my actual name

Jonathan: Well, what is "Timmy's" e-mail address? I'll hook you up.

Timmy: Timmy has placed orders using txxxxxx@gmail.com in the past

Jonathan: All right TODD!

Jonathan: ☺

Jonathan: I'm going to upgrade your account to VIP status! This will ensure that all future orders go out with 1-business-day shipping free of charge!

Jonathan: Just place your future orders at http://vip.zappos.com.

Timmy: Timmy likey!

Jonathan: Good. Good...

Jonathan: Let Jonathan know if there is anything else that Jonathan can do for Timmy.

Timmy: Ok, Timmy ok now. Timmy time to go shopping!

Jonathan: Have fun!

Be Adventurous, Creative, and Open-Minded

At Zappos, we think it's important for people and the company as a whole to be bold and daring (but not reckless). We want everyone to not be afraid to take risks and to not be afraid to make mistakes, because if people aren't making mistakes then that means they're not taking enough risks. Over time, we want everyone to develop his/her gut about business decisions. We want people to develop and improve their decision-making skills. We encourage people to make mistakes as long as they learn from them.

We never want to become complacent and accept the status quo just because that's the way things have always been done. We should always be seeking adventure and having fun exploring new possibilities. By having the freedom to be creative in our solutions, we end up making our own luck. We approach situations and challenges with an open mind.

Sometimes our sense of adventure and creativity causes us to be unconventional in our solutions (because we have the freedom to think outside the box), but that's what allows us to rise above and stay ahead of the competition.

Ask yourself: Are you taking enough risks? Are you afraid of making mistakes? Do you push yourself outside of your comfort zone? Is there a sense of adventure and creativity in the work that you do? What are some creative things that you can contribute to Zappos? Do you approach situations and challenges with an open mind?

Be Adventurous, Creative, and Open-Minded
by Christa F. (Recruiting Manager)

When I joined Zappos in December of 2004, I was leaving behind the staffing industry after eight years of working with two very large and very corporate staffing companies. In that world, Complacency and Status Quo reigned, Adventure and Fun having long ago been banished from the kingdom, if they had ever been there at all. I had been slowly descending to final burnout and had decided I never wanted to interview another person again. If you noticed my title and are thinking, "Huh, that seems… odd," don't worry, this story has a happy ending.

I saw that Zappos.com had a job opening for an HR Generalist and applied. This was *the* company everyone was talking about—the new, hip, fun, cool company that had just moved to town from San Francisco. And while that was definitely interesting and exciting, I may have mentioned I really wanted to get out of recruiting.

Somehow the stars aligned and I got the job! A few days into my second week, my manager tentatively approached me to let me know that given my background, my first big project was—drumroll please—yep, to help set up a recruiting process and start recruiting. Sigh…

You could probably guess I wasn't thrilled at first, but here's what I quickly came to realize—my problem with recruiting wasn't the actual function of recruiting, it was the lack of creativity and adventure in my work that had been "killing me softly."

At Zappos, as with all the core values, Being Adventurous, Creative, and Open-Minded is not a recommendation; it's the way we live. And if you think you can't apply this or other core values to traditionally stodgy, policy-driven, and boring departments (indeed, HR is probably at the top of that list) within your company, think again.

When we were working to create our recruiting and screening process, we were trying to figure out not only how to assess whether or not candidates would be a match with our core values, but also how we were going to demonstrate and show—infuse—our core values into our process. Talk about having to be creative, be willing to take some risks, and be open-minded!

For example, one of the biggest challenges on the plate was hiring a large volume of Customer Loyalty Team representatives very quickly. With a team of three at the time, we just weren't able to interview fast enough. Tony had a crazy idea, as he is wont to do, and suggested that instead of doing just a traditional job fair to get a lot of people in, why not do some speed dating?

My first reaction was hell no, this will never work, and I am going to need a month to figure this out and get it right. But in the spirit of being open-minded, and honestly, not having a better plan, we gave it a try. We started with the basics: We placed an ad in the paper, candidates came in to listen to a presentation on Zappos and the job details, and then they met with six Zappos employees for five minutes each to interview. Our intention was to weed out folks who definitely weren't going to be a fit quickly and then bring the rest back for sit-down interviews.

It was far from perfect but it was a start. From there, the work of fine-tuning and making the process more and more effective and Zappos-like was an exhilarating challenge. Over the year, we added things like dance music, drinks, and munchies to the presentation. We made it interactive and surprising by making it part informative, part stand-up comedy. We had folks introduce themselves to the group and share a fun fact (not a bad way to see who the outgoing leaders are in the group) and also did an "Oprah" moment where we gave away prizes (Zappos schwag) to "lucky audience members." We added an old-fashioned kitchen timer to the interview/dating part and when the five minutes was up and the candidates were moving to the next interviewer, we let them know with the buzzzzzzzzzz and a chorus of "SWITCH!!!!!"

The energy and excitement from the growing recruiting team on how to make the job fair better, more effective, more fun, and more reflective of the Zappos culture was overwhelming. It quickly spilled over into everything we did and manifested in things like themed interview rooms where candidates would be more likely to relax, respond to questions truthfully, and show their own personality and creativity.

It even showed up in new hire orientation. As part of the paperwork we cover, one deals with the expectations for the four-week new hire class—which are essentially a list of reasons a person might get fired in those first weeks. Talk about a buzz kill on the first day. Yes, the information is important and needs to be shared, but how do we do it in a Zappos way? Thanks to two loyal *Saturday Night Live* watchers on my team, we decided to "steal" a few well-known and loved characters from the show and perform skits to convey the information but in a very over-the-top and funny way.

There are many more examples I could give but suffice it to say that five years later, when I look at my team and what we have done at Zappos, I am so very proud and so very fulfilled in our work. The problem when someone feels burned out, bored, unchallenged, or stifled by their work is not the job itself but rather the environment and playground rules given to them to do the job at hand.

Let your employees take risks and try new things. Some will work and some won't and that is okay. Let your employees bring all of themselves to their job. You may have an amazingly talented software engineer who is also a rockin' musician—let him or her find an outlet for this passion at work too.

I think when people say they dread going into work on Monday morning, it's because they know they are leaving a piece of themselves at home. Why not see what happens when you challenge your employees to bring all of their talents to their job and reward them not for doing it just like everyone else, but for pushing the envelope, being adventurous, creative, and open-minded, and trying new things?

So you see, there's always a happy ending, right? I am still in recruiting, I interview people on a daily basis, and I absolutely love it!

Sample Interview Questions at Zappos

The applicant is willing to think and act outside the box.

- "Give me an example from your previous job(s) where you had to think and act outside the box."
- "What was the best mistake you made on the job? Why was it the best?"
- "Tell me about a time you recognized a problem/area to improve that was outside of your job duties and solved without being asked to. What was it, how did you do it?"

The applicant is more creative than the average person.

- "Would you say you are more or less creative than the average person? Can you give me an example?"
- "If it was your first day on the job at Zappos and your task was to make the interview/recruiting process more fun, what would you do for those eight hours?"

The applicant is willing to take risks in trying to solve a problem.

- "What's an example of a risk you took in a previous job? What was the outcome?"
- "When was the last time you broke the rules/policy to get the job done?"

Pursue Growth and Learning

At Zappos, we think it's important for employees to grow both personally and professionally. It's important to constantly challenge and stretch yourself, and not be stuck in a job where you don't feel like you are growing or learning.

We believe that inside every employee is more potential than even the employee himself/herself realizes. Our goal is to help employees unlock that potential. But it has to be a joint effort: You have to want to challenge and stretch yourself in order for it to happen.

If you've been at Zappos for more than a few months, one thing is clear: Zappos is growing. We grow because we take on new challenges, and we face even more new challenges because we're growing. It's an endless cycle, and it's a good thing: it's the only way for a company to survive. But it can also at times feel risky, stressful, and confusing.

Sometimes it may seem that new problems crop up as fast as we solve the old ones (sometimes faster!), but that just means that we're moving—that we're getting better and stronger. Anyone who wants to compete with us has to learn the same things, so problems are just mile markers. Each one we pass means we've gotten better.

Yet no matter how much better we get, we'll always have hard work to do, we'll never be done, and we'll never "get it right."

That may seem negative, but it's not: we'll do our best to "get it right," and then do it again when we find out that things have changed. That is the cycle of growth, and like it or not, that cycle won't stop.

It's hard...but if we weren't doing something hard, then we'd have no business. The only reason we aren't swamped by our competition is because what we do is hard, and we do it better than anyone else. If it ever gets too easy, start looking for a tidal wave of competition to wash us away.

It may seem sometimes like we don't know what we're doing. And it's true: we don't. That's a bit scary, but you can take comfort in knowing that nobody else knows how to do what we're doing either. If they did, they'd be the Web's most popular shoe store. Sure, people have done parts of what we do before, but what we've learned over the years at Zappos is that the devil is in the details. And that's where we're breaking new ground.

So there are no experts in what we're doing. Except for us: we are becoming experts as we do this. And for anyone we bring on board, the best expertise they can bring is expertise at learning and adapting and figuring new things out—helping the company grow, and in the process they will also be growing themselves.

Ask yourself: How do you grow personally? How do you grow professionally? Are you a better person today than you were yesterday? How do you get your co-workers and direct reports to grow personally? How do you get your co-workers and direct reports to grow professionally? How do you challenge and stretch yourself? Are you learning something every day? What is your vision for where you want to go? How do you get the company as a whole to grow? Are you doing everything you can to promote company growth, and at the same time are you helping others understand the growth? Do you understand the company vision?

Pursue Growth and Learning
by Maura S.

When I began working at Zappos six years ago, I had no plans to make it a career. I happened to live in San Francisco, trying to get a full-time job in the museum world. It wasn't working out too well, so I applied to answer phones so I could pay rent.

Looking back, it was simply a job. Now that job has turned into something so much more meaningful.

I knew Zappos was a great place to work right away because of two things: the great people I got to spend my day with, and their fantastic philosophy on customer service. But I don't really think I understood how special this company was until I made a huge leap of faith and moved with them to Las Vegas in April 2004.

The Zappos Core Values were sent out to us in 2006. We knew we had a unique culture and now we had something to reference, something that we all contributed to, something to which we said, "Yes! This is what we believe in."

The Core Values weren't just for the office; they were a way of life. I loved and identified with them all, but I immediately honed in on Core Value 5: Pursue Growth and Learning.

By that time I had been with the company two and a half years. In that short time I had been pushed into management positions, when I had no experience and wasn't looking for that in a job. In hindsight, I'm thankful they pushed me there.

I knew that Zappos trusted me, maybe even before I could trust myself in certain roles. Because of that, I was able to learn and grow by leaps and bounds, both personally and professionally.

After the core values came out, I really started to "pursue" all of the growth and learning around me. I realized how lucky I was to work in such a supportive environment, where I could come up with ideas and know I've been already given the go-ahead to "just do."

I became more confident and sure of my role as a leader in the company. I pushed myself to start speaking on behalf of Zappos at conferences, something that I would've been horrified to do five years ago. Now I love it.

I was learning and growing not only within the Zappos walls, but also in my personal life. I was able to set goals and buy a house on my own. As a kid I was an avid reader, but in college I lost my zest for reading. Now I can't keep up with all the wonderful books out there.

I've also pushed myself to get back into a healthy lifestyle. I've run five half marathons and am currently training for my first full in December (sponsored by Zappos!). I've traveled to Asia to go scuba diving, Central America to climb a volcano, and camped on one to watch the neighboring one erupt. Happiness!

It's amazing to look back on the last six years and imagine the twenty-five-year-old I was, and see how much I've grown and changed. Zappos has been a huge part of that growth and every day I walk in to work, I can't wait to learn more.

Build Open and Honest Relationships With Communication

Fundamentally, we believe that openness and honesty make for the best relationships because that leads to trust and faith. We value strong relationships in all areas: with managers, direct reports, customers (internal and external), vendors, business partners, team members, and co-workers.

Strong, positive relationships that are open and honest are a big part of what differentiates Zappos from most other companies. Strong relationships allow us to accomplish much more than we would be able to otherwise.

A key ingredient in strong relationships is to develop emotional connections. It's important to always act with integrity in your relationships, to be compassionate, friendly, loyal, and to make sure that you do the right thing and treat your relationships well. The hardest thing to do is to build trust, but if the trust exists, you can accomplish so much more.

In any relationship, it's important to be a good listener as well as a good communicator. Open, honest communication is the best foundation for any relationship, but remember that at the end of the day it's not what you say or what you do, but how you make people feel that matters the most. In order for someone to feel good about a relationship, they must know that the other person truly cares about them, both personally and professionally.

At Zappos, we embrace diversity in thoughts, opinions, and backgrounds. The more widespread and diverse your relationships are, the bigger the positive impact you can make on the company, and the more valuable you will be to the company. It is critical for relationship-building to have effective, open, and honest communication.

As the company grows, communication becomes more and more important, because everyone needs to understand how his/her team connects to the big picture of what we're trying to accomplish.

Communication is always one of the weakest spots in any organization, no matter how good the communication is. We want everyone to always try to go the extra mile in encouraging thorough, complete, and effective communication.

Ask yourself: How much do people enjoy working with you? How can you improve those relationships? What new relationships can you build throughout the company beyond just the co-workers that you work with on a daily basis? How do you WOW the people that you have relationships with? How can you make your relationships more open and honest? How can you do a better job of communicating with everyone?

ZAPPOS COMMUNICATION POLICY
BE REAL AND USE YOUR BEST JUDGMENT!

Build a Positive Team and Family Spirit

At Zappos, we place a lot of emphasis on our culture because we are both a team and a family. We want to create an environment that is friendly, warm, and exciting. We encourage diversity in ideas, opinions, and points of view.

The best leaders are those that lead by example and are both team followers as well as team leaders. We believe that in general, the best ideas and decisions are made from the bottom up, meaning by those on the front lines that are closest to the issues and/or the customers. The role of a manager is to remove obstacles and enable his/her direct reports to succeed. This means the best leaders are servant-leaders. They serve those they lead.

The best team members take initiative when they notice issues so that the team and the company can succeed. The best team members take ownership of issues and collaborate with other team members whenever challenges arise.

The best team members have a positive influence on one another and everyone they encounter. They strive to eliminate any kind of cynicism and negative interactions. Instead, the best team members are those that strive to create harmony with each other and whoever else they interact with.

We believe that the best teams are those that not only work with each other, but also interact with each other outside the office environment. Many of the company's best ideas have been the direct result of informal interactions outside of the office.

For example, the idea for our culture book came about from a casual discussion outside the office.

We are more than just a team, though—we are a family. We watch out for each other, care for each other, and go above and beyond for each other because we believe in each other and we trust each other. We work together but we also play together. Our bonds go far beyond the typical "co-worker" relationships found at most other companies.

Ask yourself: How do you encourage more teamwork? How do you encourage more people to take initiative? How do you encourage more people to take ownership? What can you do with your team members so that you feel both like a family and a team? How can you build stronger relationships with your team members both inside and outside the office? Do you instill a sense of team and family not just within your department, but across the entire company? Do you exemplify a positive team spirit?

Build a Positive Team and Family Spirit
by Robin P.

My husband passed away under tragic circumstances in December of 2007. I couldn't begin to think of what that was going to mean for our children, our family, or for me.

When I first heard the news, I was numb, but I needed to make a call. Strangely enough, the call wasn't to an immediate family member. It was to my employer, Zappos.com. That one action made me realize the strong connection I felt with my co-workers and the Zappos culture. It essentially was my home away from home.

When my senior manager received my hysterical call, she showed great compassion and gave sound advice to calm me. She assured that I shouldn't be concerned with anything else but to take care of myself and my family, and that—day or night—I should call if I needed anything. After she gave me every single one of her phone numbers, I knew she meant it.

As much as Zappos meant to me before, the things they did after my husband passed amazed and humbled me. I was reassured that I shouldn't feel pressure to return to work as soon as possible. They even volunteered to cater the reception for my husband's service. My visiting family had never heard of these kinds of gestures given by a workplace. I just smiled and said, "Wonderful. That's what Zappos is."

When I returned to work, I was nervous, unsure of how my co-workers would act around me. But I wasn't anxious for long. There was always someone there to listen, offer consoling words, sit with me as I released my tears, or just give a hug. Co-workers and managers alike allowed me time to heal and gave me the strength I needed to continue as a contributing and functioning member of the team.

In the end, the most important contributions from my extended family at Zappos were support and friendship. Zappos was my refuge and healing place that gave me everything I needed to continue on with my life.

Do More with Less

Zappos has always been about being able to do more with less. While we may be casual in our interactions with each other, we are focused and serious about the operations of our business. We believe in hard work and putting in the extra effort to get things done.

We believe in operational excellence, and realize that there is always room for improvement in everything we do. This means that our work is never done. In order to stay ahead of the competition (or would-be competition), we need to continuously innovate as well as make incremental improvements to our operations, always striving to make ourselves more efficient, always trying to figure out how to do something better. We use mistakes as learning opportunities.

We must never lose our sense of urgency in making improvements. We must never settle for "good enough," because good is the enemy of great, and our goal is to not only become a great company, but to become the greatest service company in the world. We set and exceed our own high standards, constantly raising the bar for competitors and for ourselves.

Ask yourself: How can you do what you're doing more efficiently? How can your department become more efficient? How can the company as a whole become more efficient? How can you personally help the company become more efficient?

Do More with Less
by Vanessa L.

I joined Zappos in 2007 during a hard patch in my life. I went to a temp agency looking for work and was told there was a company that might fit me really well. The minute I walked through those doors, my life had changed.

I remember thinking the core values were simple, easy to follow, and incredibly impactful. Of the ten, I've integrated "Do More With Less" into my life in the most ways.

Around my first Christmas working at Zappos, I had no family, no car, no phone, no money, and nowhere to go for the holidays. In my stubborn head I wanted to enjoy Christmas, even if it was all by myself. I decided I'd walk to the store and buy one small holiday item every day until Christmas Eve, and then I'd cook up a little feast for myself.

I ended up buying two yams on sale for 39 cents. That was as far as my shopping went. Christmas Eve came and I made my yams. I had neither spices nor even a pan in which to cook them. I found some tinfoil to use instead.

Opening up my cabinet, I saw a package of hot cocoa powder with marshmallows. I sifted the package, picked out all the little marshmallows, cleansed them in water, and put them in the yams for flavor.

I ate it all, even though it was not tasty. But the funny thing was…I was so incredibly happy in that moment. I'll never forget how content I felt that night. I could've been miserable and cried myself to sleep because I was alone during the holidays, a time I'm used to spending with family and a whole table full of food.

I felt Do More With Less got me through rough patches in life and made me think outside the box in my personal and professional life. There's never one way to do things, but an incredible amount of ways to get things done. It takes an open and creative mind to find, invent, and execute them. I've been more creative, passionate, and resourceful here at Zappos than anywhere else.

Roadblocks aren't a dead end here. They're a welcome challenge.

Thinking back to when I made those yams years ago, doing more with less, I now know that any issue arising in life is a welcome challenge where I can learn and grow. Since that time, I've gained back material possessions like a phone, car, home, and steady supply of groceries (including yams!).

I know it's not material possessions that generate my happiness but one thing I have to admit...I still enjoy yams with freeze-dried marshmallows in packets!

Be Passionate and Determined

Passion is the fuel that drives ourselves and our company forward. We value passion, determination, perseverance, and the sense of urgency.

We are inspired because we believe in what we are doing and where we are going. We don't take "no" or "that'll never work" for an answer, because if we had, Zappos would never have started in the first place.

Passion and determination are contagious. We believe in having a positive and optimistic (but realistic) attitude about everything we do, because we realize that this inspires others to have the same attitude.

There is excitement in knowing that everyone you work with has a tremendous impact on a larger dream and vision, and you can see that impact day in and day out.

Ask yourself: Are you passionate about the company? Are you passionate about your work? Do you love what you do and who you work with? Are you happy here? Are you inspired? Do you believe in what we are doing and where we are going? Is this the place for you?

Be Passionate and Determined
by Dr. Vik

I met with one of our Customer Loyalty reps a couple of years back. She was young, twenty-one to be exact, and was tired of throwing her money down the tubes in an apartment she was renting. So she set her sights on buying a house.

She and her husband had bills and credit cards piled so high, they didn't have much left over. All they could save was $25 a month toward the purchase of their future house. As little as that was, we decided it was the routine of saving that was the most important thing. So they began at a starting point that was manageable, and not so aggressive they'd want to quit.

After the thirty days were up, she told me it was so easy to save the $25, she wanted to raise the amount. And since her new routine of saving was pretty easy, they decided they'd start making a dent in other bills they had, like student loans. Albeit change wasn't felt overnight, they started to make headway and progress was made just the same.

She'd give updates every so often and one day, after a couple of years had passed, she came in to tell me all their bills were paid off and they had just purchased a new home. Some time after, they even bought a boat for recreation.

Their success wasn't immediate but her passion and determination to work their plan were impressive to say the least. Her takeaway from the whole process is that they were in total control of their future and their life—they just needed to make a plan of their own choosing, and work it through to completion.

Be Humble

While we have grown quickly in the past, we recognize that there are always challenges ahead to tackle. We believe that no matter what happens, we should always be respectful of everyone.

While we celebrate our individual and team successes, we are not arrogant nor do we treat others differently from how we would want to be treated. Instead, we carry ourselves with a quiet confidence, because we believe that in the long run our character will speak for itself.

Ask yourself: Are you humble when talking about your accomplishments? Are you humble when talking about the company's accomplishments? Do you treat both large and small vendors with the same amount of respect that they treat you?

It's more fun to talk with someone who doesn't use long difficult words but rather short easy words like "What about lunch?"
—Winnie-the-Pooh

One of our other goals when we came up with our ten core values was to create a list that was unique to Zappos and didn't sound like every other company. No two company cultures are exactly alike, yet the core values for a lot of corporations sound very similar. In most cases, you wouldn't be able to identify the company just by looking at their list of core values.

Doing a Google search for each of your company's core values can serve as a good test for whether your company's core values are unique. If you Google any of our core values, you'll find that Zappos always shows up somewhere, and in most cases we are the number one search result.

Ultimately, though, it's not the Google search results that matter. What matters is that each of the core values becomes a natural part of employees' everyday language and way of thinking. Committable core values that are truly integrated into a company's operations can align an entire organization and serve as a guide for employees to make their own decisions.

I'm not suggesting that other companies should adopt our core values at Zappos. In most cases, that would be a huge mistake. Our core values are simply the core values that make sense for us.

In the books *Good to Great* and *Tribal Leadership*, the authors looked at what characteristics separated the great companies from the good ones. One of the most important ingredients they found was a strong company culture. Core values are essentially a formalized definition of a company's culture.

As it turns out, it doesn't actually matter *what* your company's core values are. What matters is that you have them and that you commit to them. What's important is the alignment that you get from them when they become the default way of thinking for the entire organization.

Your personal core values define who you are, and a company's core values ultimately define the company's character and brand.

For individuals, character is destiny.
For organizations, culture is destiny.

To learn more about how you can create committable core values for your organization, take a look at the links in the Appendix of this book.

Vendor Relations
by Fred

I consider vendor relationships to be one of the key components to Zappos's success. Without them, we wouldn't be where we are today. To give some perspective, it can be helpful to start from the beginning, and in this case, it began with a background check.

My career in retail began in Bellevue, Washington, on the men's shoe floor at Nordstrom. Over the course of eight years,

I worked my way up through the ranks until I achieved a buyer role in San Francisco, in one of the largest stores in the company. While there, I worked with many buyers of varying styles and interacted with many vendors. I witnessed some ugly and adversarial relationships; I witnessed some positive and collaborative relationships. And, contrary to popular belief, it was the nice guys who always came out on top.

I was still at Nordstrom on that fateful day in 1999 when I answered the call from Nick. I had lunch with Nick, Tony, and Alfred at Mel's Diner to discuss the potential of creating direct (drop ship) relationships with footwear vendors to sell shoes online. At the time, this was a novel concept and a bit risky. Nordstrom was a stable company, and I had a good job, but being the gambling man that I am, I decided to bet it all on the opportunity to help build something from the ground up. I took a leap of faith.

I knew from the beginning that we needed to have strong and positive partnerships with our vendors in order to be successful. At Nordstrom, I saw buyers abuse their vendors daily and use their positions of power for short-term wins; these buyers ultimately failed in the long run. Then there were the buyers who partnered closely with their vendors, treated them with respect, and created long-term opportunities; these buyers always had the best business. I decided early in my career that I would create relationships and opportunities that would stand the test of time, and I was fortunate that I could rely on many of the relationships I'd already built.

The typical industry approach is to treat vendors like the enemy. Show them no respect, don't return their phone calls, make them wait for scheduled appointments, and make them buy the meals. Scream at them, blame them, abuse them... anything to get as much as possible and squeeze out every last dime. In fact, I know of a time when, after a vendor sold to an independent's competitor, the buyer became so upset that he literally pulled down his pants and demanded the vendor kiss his ass!

It's a wonder people don't realize that business doesn't have to be done this way. Ultimately, each party is out for the same thing: to take care of the customers, grow the business, and be profitable. In the long run, it doesn't behoove either party if there's only one winner. If vendors can't make a profit then they don't have money to invest in research and development, which in turn means that the products they bring to market will be less inspiring to customers, which in turn detriments the retailer's business because customers aren't inspired to buy. People want to cut costs and negotiate aggressively because there's a limited amount of profit to be shared by both sides. As a result of this "death spiral," most retailers fail.

We wanted Zappos to be different by creating collaborative relationships in which both parties share the risks, as well as the rewards. We found it much easier to create alliances when partners align themselves to the same vision and commit to accountability, knowing we'll all benefit from achieving our goals. Not only does this approach get both sides pulling in the same direction, it creates an environment and culture where people are inspired to get up every day, passionate for what they do. It creates empowerment and control of the business, as well as a sense of pride and ownership. It makes people want to do more because they know their contribution means something.

We implement this partnership mentality in many ways at Zappos, but it all begins with the Golden Rule: Treat others as you'd like to be treated. When vendors fly to visit our offices in Las Vegas, they are greeted at the airport by one of our Zappos shuttles. When they arrive at our offices, their buyer welcomes them as we take their sample bags off their hands so we can deliver them to the meeting room. If it's their first time visiting our office, we give them a tour. We offer them drinks and snacks, basically anything we can do to make them feel comfortable. This is all far from industry standard, but if we were in their position, I'm sure we wouldn't mind being treated this way.

The same mentality applies to communication with our vendors. If they call, we try to return their call the same day. If they e-mail, we try to respond within a few hours. We realize the importance of communication, and if our partners are trying to reach us, we need to be responsive. Our customers expect this type of responsiveness from us, and so should our vendors.

Early on in Zappos, because of the size of our business, we realized we were going to need help running it. There was just no way we could afford to staff all the buyers needed to manage the number of styles and sizes in our selection. I'll never forget the afternoon I turned my chair around and asked Tony what he thought about giving vendors access to the same information as our buyers. Traditionally in retail, information is hoarded, kept secret, and used as leverage against the vendors to get more out of them. Retailers wouldn't want a vendor to know how well they're doing so they can demand more. But if we created true transparency in our business, not only would they help us, they'd benefit as well.

Not too long after I proposed the idea to Tony, he spun back around and said, "Were you thinking about something like this?" He created the beginning of what we now refer to as "the extranet." It does exactly what we had discussed. It allows the vendors complete visibility into our business. They're able to see inventory levels, sales, and profitability. They can write suggested orders for our buyers to approve. They can communicate with our creative team and make changes to their brand boutiques on the site. In effect, they're given the keys to the shop.

Why do we do this? The average buyer at Zappos has a portfolio of fifty brands, but because of transparency, there's an additional fifty pairs of eyes helping run the business too. Not only that, vendors are the experts at what they do. No one buyer knows a brand better than the brand's own representative. So why not leverage their knowledge to help us run a better business? As a result, when they feel empowered to manage their own business using the tools and accessibility we provide, they'll spend more hours helping us than their typical account. The success of our team can be attributed to our buyers and vendor partners, together.

Negotiations at Zappos are a bit different as well. Instead of pounding the vendors, we collaborate. If we're looking for longer payment terms, we'll present different sales plans based on the days-of-payment terms. We decide together what makes the most sense for the business, the amount of risk we want to sign up for, and how quickly we want the business to grow. We approach marketing from a similar standpoint as well. We collaborate on what both of our brands are trying to achieve and what it will take us to get there. We don't believe that negotiations need to be an arm-wrestling match. If both parties are honest about our positions and objectives, we should be able to find an equitable way to get there.

We know there's no way we could've achieved our success as a company without our vendors' commitment and passion, so every year, we like to show a little gratitude. We take over a venue such as the Hard Rock Hotel pool or Rain Nightclub at the Palms and invite all of our vendors (over one thousand) to our annual Vendor Appreciation Party. Between our vendors and the Zappos team, we have over three-thousand people on hand. We time it around the World Shoe Association convention and love it when people tell us it's the highlight of the show. We cater food, beverages, and wildly interesting entertainment (goats in tutus, dancers, little people, fire eaters…you name it, we've probably had it!) with the hope they realize how much they mean to our company. The first year we did it, the vendor community was so blown away by the gesture, they talked about it for months! Now it's become such an event that vendors we don't work with and other retailers try to sneak in so they can enjoy the fun too.

We like to show our appreciation other times of the year too. When a brand achieves certain levels of sales, we print T-shirts for them that read: MY BRAND DID A MILLION DOLLARS OF SALES ON ZAPPOS. COM. When we dine with vendors, we always try to pick up the check. This rarely happens in the retail world, but it's our way to WOW them as much as we try to WOW our customers. Picking up the check at dinner has actually become a competition with many of our vendors. Not too long ago, a group of us went to dinner with Rob Schmertz and Steve Madden, and because they had been so shocked when we'd picked up dinner the last time, they called ahead and made arrangements to get the check and warn the restaurant that we'd try to play tricks to get it! It rarely happens, but they scooped us!

On the last Friday of every month, Zappos also throws a golf tournament where we invite our vendors to play with us. As some say, more work gets done on the golf course than in the office. Case in point, we actually got into the eyewear category due to a conversation with our Oakley rep, Paul, after a round of golf. Today, our eyewear category is one of the largest online, but it may have never happened if we hadn't been out building relationships with our vendors.

Our relationships aren't limited to just the retail industry either. Our long-standing relationship with UPS has led to partnerships in finding new and unique ways to WOW our customers. They've been a critical part of our growth from day one, and even though we were an insignificant part of their business at the beginning, they always treated us with respect. Our long-time rep Alex works tirelessly on our behalf to find new and innovative ways to improve our service. He and UPS took the time to immerse themselves in our culture and consequently, he's not only our representative, he's a friend.

There are far too many vendors to name them all, but we're also very fortunate in our partnership with Wells Fargo. When others doubted, they extended us a line of credit in a critical point in our growth. They always work with us to continue to build our business and invest the time to know us personally. They're passionate about our business and took the time to understand it.

The benefits we've reaped from concentrating on building relationships with our vendors are endless. They help us plan our businesses and make sure we have enough of the right product at the right time. When inventory's scarce, they help procure inventory on hot-selling items. Sometimes they provide unique items that can only be found on Zappos. They work closely with our marketing team to plan the right campaigns, making sure we're in the right places. We get involved in decisions regarding the direction of their lines. In fact, one of the biggest innovations of our extranet came to be because of a suggestion from our Clarks representative, Tom. Tom observed that the extranet would be much easier if photographs of the styles were available, and it was a lightbulb moment. Today, this feature of the extranet is most helpful for not only our vendors but our buying team as well!

Because of our relationships, vendors we're not currently working with are eager to partner with us. We have many brands on our site that customers can't find anywhere else online, and it's because of the trust we've built in the industry over the past ten years. Brands know and recognize we have the highest standards of maintaining their brand integrity and because of it, many only felt comfortable doing business with us.

Most importantly, I think of our vendors as friends. We enjoy each other's company, spend time together outside the work environment, and genuinely care about one another. We respect and value our relationships, and want to see each other do well. I've known many of the people I work with for almost my entire career.

When I left Nordstrom to help start Zappos and solicit brands, it was a risky proposition. At the time, we were in a channel no one thought would work, with a company no one had ever heard of. But they supported it and were willing to put their necks on the line because of the relationship we'd built over the years. Without those friendships and their belief in us, there might not be a Zappos today. Those relationships were, and continue to be, one of the most valuable parts of our business.

Layoffs

2008 was a crazy year. We experienced some of our highest highs as well as some of our lowest lows, both inside and outside of Zappos.

We began the year celebrating our prior year's financial performance. We had exceeded our 2007 operating profit goals, so we decided to surprise all of our employees with a onetime cash bonus equal to 10 percent of their annual salary. It was our way of thanking everyone for helping us exceed our goals.

Later that year, UPS invited Alfred and me to Beijing to watch the Olympics, which turned out to be an amazing experience.

Then the stock market and housing market collapsed. As the global economy tanked toward the end of 2008, our growth rate slowed. Even though we were still growing, we realized that our expenses were too high for the revenues we were bringing in. We had planned on faster growth and instead found that we had over-hired. I was amazed that things had changed very quickly.

Just eight months after giving everyone their surprise bonus, we made the tough decision to lay off 8 percent of our staff. It was one of the hardest decisions we ever had to make for the company.

Rather than trying to spin the story as a "strategic restructuring" as many other corporations were doing, we stuck by our core values and remained open and honest, not only with our employees, but with the press as well.

I sent the following e-mail to all of our employees, which we also publicly posted on our blogs:

Date: November 6, 2008
From: Tony Hsieh
To: All Zappos Employees
Subject: Update
To all Zappos employees:
    Today has been a tough, emotional day for everyone at Zappos. We made the hard choice of laying off about

8% of our employees. The layoffs will affect almost every single department at Zappos. In addition, we are also looking at closing some of our brick and mortar outlet stores in Nevada and Kentucky.

This is one of the hardest decisions we've had to make over the past 9.5 years, but we believe that it is the right decision for the long term health of the company. The rest of this email will explain why...

We feel fortunate that we have Sequoia Capital as an investor who had the foresight to see the ramifications of the tough economic times that lie ahead for all of us. On October 7, Sequoia held a meeting for all of their portfolio companies (including Zappos), with one very clear message: Cut expenses as much as possible and get to profitability and cash flow positive as soon as possible.

Jason Calacanis also has a well-written email that talks about avoiding the "death spiral," which I highly recommend reading.

Fortunately for Zappos, we're in a much better position than many other companies. Unlike many other companies, we are still growing and already profitable and cash flow positive.

And we are also fortunate that we have a revolving line of credit from Wells Fargo, US Bank, and KeyBank. This line of credit has given us a lot of financial flexibility. However, given the current economic uncertainty, we believe it's prudent to reduce our reliance on debt financing.

We've decided the right thing to do for the company is to be proactive instead of reactive. We are proactively cutting back some of our expenses today so that we can take care of our employees properly, instead of being reactive and waiting until we are forced to cut expenses.

Because we are still growing and are already profitable, we do not have to take as drastic of a step as most other companies of our size. Last year, we did $840 mm in gross merchandise sales, and this year we are forecasting to do about $1 billion in gross merchandise sales. However, when we first put together our 2008 plan at the end of 2007, we were expecting our gross merchandise sales to be even higher than $1 billion.

Because of all this, we are reducing our staff by 8%, but because we are being proactive instead of reactive about it, we are able to take care of our employees and offer them more than the standard 2 weeks severance (or no severance) that most other companies are giving.

We are offering to pay each laid-off employee through the end of the year (about 2 months), and offering an additional amount for employees that have been with us for 3 or more years.

In addition, because our regular health benefits cover 100% medical, dental, and vision for employees and 50% for spouses and dependents, we decided to offer to reimburse laid-off employees for up to 6 months of COBRA payments.

In doing all of this to take care of laid-off employees, we expect that it will actually increase, not decrease, our costs for 2008, but we feel this is the right thing to do for our employees. It will put us in the position of having a lot more financial flexibility in being able to respond to potential changes in the economy in 2009.

E-commerce growth has slowed compared to its growth rate a year ago, but the good news is that even in this tough economic environment, e-commerce overall is still growing.

Within the footwear category, we are the online market leader. When times are tough, the strongest players in any market have an opportunity to gain even more market share, even if overall growth may be slower. Historically, we have actually grown faster than the overall e-commerce market, and we anticipate for that to continue in 2009.

For the rest of 2008 as well as for 2009, we anticipate continuing to grow year over year. Our current forecasts are that we will continue to be profitable and cash flow positive, as long as we are proactive instead of reactive in managing our business and financials.

I know that many tears were shed today, both by laid-off and non-laid-off employees alike. Given our family culture, our layoffs are much tougher emotionally than they would be at many other companies.

I've been asked by some employees whether it's okay to Twitter about what's going on. Our Twitter policy remains the same as it's always been: just be real, and use your best judgment.

These are tough times for everyone, and I'm sure there will be many follow-up questions to this email. If you have any questions about your specific job or department, please talk to your department manager. For all other questions, comments, or thoughts, please feel free to email me.

—Tony Hsieh, CEO

After the weekend had passed, I sent a follow up e-mail to our remaining employees, which we also publicly posted on our blogs:

Date: November 11, 2008
From: Tony Hsieh
To: All Zappos Employees
Subject: Moving forward

Last week was a tough week for everyone, as we went through the process of laying off 8% of the Zappos family. At the same time, it was also heartwarming hearing all the stories of Zappos employees and ex-employees getting together for drinks Thursday night after the layoffs as well as over the weekend.

The economic environment we're in right now is unlike any we've ever witnessed in our lifetime. These are extraordinary times, and America is not out of the woods yet. Many people expect 2–3 million Americans to lose their jobs before we hit the bottom of our current economic cycle.

As difficult as times may be, if there's one thing I've learned in life, it's that things are never as bad as they seem or as good as they seem. In most cases, this perspective usually comes long after a "bad" or "good" event has occurred.

This is actually the second time we've had to do layoffs across the board at Zappos. We've been around for 9.5 years, and the first time we had to do layoffs was during the early years of the company, when we laid off about half our staff due to a bad economy and our inability to raise funding. At the time, we still were not profitable.

However, the layoffs we did in the early days forced the team that remained to become much stronger, and because we did not have a lot of money at the time, it forced us to focus on servicing our existing customers instead of trying to acquire a lot of new customers. Ultimately, it was the catalyst for transforming Zappos from being just about shoes to a company focused on customer service and company culture. It started a domino effect that ultimately made us who we are today.

Moving forward, we have a similar opportunity. We have the opportunity to make our culture stronger than ever before. It's something that will require everyone's involvement and effort, but based on our history, I know it can be done.

We also have the opportunity to make the company healthier than ever before. As we come up with innovative and creative ways of generating more revenue, profits, and cash flow, we will be prioritizing them based on what will be most beneficial to our company.

One question that has come up is whether we will be doing another round of layoffs after the new year. There are currently no plans to do so. When we laid off 8% of our employees last week, we chose that number because we felt that it would cut our expenses enough to get us through all of 2009, based on our current financial forecasts. As mentioned in my previous email, our layoffs were done proactively to ensure that we would be profitable and cash flow positive in 2009.

As part of reducing our 2009 expenses, and to bring us all closer together, we are in the process of moving people so that everyone in our Las Vegas offices will be either in the 2280 or 2290 building, which are next door to each other. The moving should be completed over the next couple of weeks.

We've got a busy holiday season ahead, and while everyone will be busy and working hard with their individual jobs, let's also make a conscious effort to think about how we can help each other out even more than usual—not just within your department, but cross-departmentally and throughout the entire company as well.

Remember, this is not my company, and this is not our investors' company. This company is all of ours, and it's up to all of us where we go from here. The power lies in each and every one of us to move forward and come out as a team stronger than we've ever been in the history of the company.

Let's show the world what Zappos is capable of.
—Tony Hsieh, CEO

We received a lot of media attention because we had been so public and transparent with our layoffs instead of trying to keep everything quiet. Going through such a dark period of time in the public eye really put our culture to the test. But as with all challenges, our employees figured out how to get through things and move on.

Looking back now, I'm incredibly thankful and grateful that we all banded together and made sure that we didn't lose our team and family spirit. It really makes me feel proud of our employees.

I also hope that we never have to go through anything like that ever again.

Pipeline

Many corporations like to say that their people are their most important asset. There are a few problems with that approach.

First, as soon as someone leaves, you've lost an asset. Second, if the company grows, then there may come a time later down the line when the company outgrows an employee because the employee still has the same skill set that he had when he first joined. When that happens, usually the solution in a lot of other companies is to bring in a more experienced employee from outside the company, which presents a third challenge: That new employee often may not be a culture fit.

Our philosophy at Zappos is different. Rather than focusing on individuals as assets, we instead focus on building as our asset a *pipeline* of people in every single department with varying levels of skills and experience, ranging from entry level all the way up through senior management and leadership positions. Our vision is for almost all of our hires to be entry level, but for the company to provide all the training and mentorship necessary so that any employee has the opportunity to become a senior leader within the company within five to seven years. For us, this is still a work in progress, but we're really excited about its future.

Without continually growing and learning both personally and professionally, it's unlikely that any individual employee will still be with the company ten years from now. Our goal at Zappos is for our employees to think of their work not as a job or career, but as a calling.

Our pipeline strategy started when we first moved to Vegas in 2004. Even though Vegas was great for hiring for our call center, we found it challenging to convince merchandisers and buyers who had years of industry experience to move from places such as Los Angeles or New York to Las Vegas. So we decided to start training and growing our own merchants from the ground up.

Today, nearly all of the hires for our merchandising department are for entry-level merchandising assistants. We have a three-year merchant development program where merchandising assistants are trained, certified, and given increasing portfolio responsibilities as well as put into management and leadership roles.

At the entry level, all we really care about is if they are passionate about the category of product their team is responsible for. For our couture team, we hire people who love reading fashion magazines. For our running team, we hire marathoners. For our outdoors team, we hire people who regularly go hiking and camping on weekends.

Over a three-year period, merchandising assistants are promoted to assistant buyers and then to buyers. (After three years, they can go on to become senior buyers, directors, and eventually VPs.)

Our pipeline philosophy has been incredibly successful within our merchandising department, and we've spent the past year working on rolling out similar programs for all of our departments.

There are specific training programs that are unique to each department, but we also have a Pipeline Team that offers courses for all departments. Many of the courses are required in order for an employee to be promoted to certain levels within the company, regardless of which department he or she may be in.

A Sampling of Courses Offered by the Pipeline Team

- Four-week new hire training (including answering phones)
- Zappos History
- Zappos Culture
- Communication 1
- Communication 2
- Communication 3
- Intro to Coaching
- Zappos Library: *Fred Factor* and *Fish*
- Intro to Finance
- Science of Happiness 101
- Tribal Leadership
- 1-week Kentucky Boot Camp

- New manager orientation
- Performance Enhancement
- HR 101
- HR 102
- Leadership Essentials
- Zappos Library: *Made to Stick*
- Finance 2: The Planning Process
- Public Speaking
- Delivering Happiness
- Intermediate-Level Competency with Microsoft Office
- Grammar and Writing 1
- Grammar and Writing 2
- Stress Management
- Time Management
- WOWing Through Tours
- Customer Loyalty Skills Refresher
- Progression Plan Workshop

Once our pipeline is filled for every department, then any-time a single individual leaves the company, there will always be someone right in front of him and someone right behind him in the pipeline to take over his responsibilities. In this way, the pipeline becomes the true asset of the company, not any single individual.

Over the longer term, we are also planning on extending the pipeline concept up to four years *before* an entry-level employee joins Zappos. If our recruiting team can start building relation-ships with college students when they first start as freshmen, and offer summer internship positions at Zappos during their time in school, then by the time they graduate from college, both sides will have a pretty good idea of whether Zappos is the right fit for the student.

Once our entire eleven-year pipeline is built (from four years prior to joining Zappos all the way through seven years after joining Zappos), we'll have a substantial long-term competitive advantage over everyone else. Combined with our ongoing efforts to grow our brand and our culture, we believe that our BCP (Brand, Culture, Pipeline) strategy will provide the platform necessary for Zappos to be a long-term enduring and growing business.

Tweets to Live By

- "Everybody has their own private Mount Everest they were put on this earth to climb."
  —Hugh MacLeod

- "If you have more than 3 priorities then you don't have any."
  —Jim Collins

- "If the person you're talking to isn't listening, be patient. Maybe he has a small piece of fluff in his ear."
  —Winnie-the-Pooh

- "In the pursuit of knowledge, something is added every day. In the pursuit of enlightenment, something is dropped every day."
  —Lao-tzu

- "Someone broke into my car last night. Nothing worth taking, car is actually less of a mess now. I should schedule this monthly."

PROFITS, PASSION, AND PURPOSE

6

Taking It to the Next Level

PR and Public Speaking

In the two years leading up to the announcement of the Amazon acquisition, Zappos started getting more and more media coverage. A lot of people assumed that we must have stepped up our PR efforts, but that wasn't the case at all. We simply continued doing what we had always done: constantly improving the customer experience while simultaneously strengthening our culture.

The funny thing is that a lot of the press we got was for things we had first done several years earlier, such as paying employees to quit during their new hire training or occasionally sending flowers to customers. We didn't intend for any of the things we were doing to end up in the news or on blogs. But every once in a while, a reporter or popular blogger would pick up on something that we were doing, and the story would spread like wildfire. We were as surprised as anyone else by the publicity because it was never planned for on our end.

We learned a great lesson: If you just focus on making sure that your product or service continually WOWs people, eventually the press will find out about it. You don't need to put a lot of effort into reaching out to the press if your company naturally creates interesting stories as a by-product of delivering a great product or experience.

As our media coverage increased, I started receiving more and more speaking requests for different conferences and industry events. One of my first speeches was at the Footwear News CEO Summit in 2005. I remember I was a nervous wreck, because I hadn't really done much public speaking before. At the time, I agreed to do it because it would be a good opportunity to tell the Zappos story to a lot of footwear vendors we were still trying to establish relationships with.

I wrote out my entire speech beforehand, and then spent a month memorizing it and rehearsing it. I couldn't sleep the night before my speech. It ended up going okay, and I was relieved when it was finally over so I could catch up on my sleep. Even though I didn't really enjoy the whole experience, it had a very positive impact on our business, so I was glad I had done it.

Over the next year, a few more speaking requests started trickling in. I agreed to all of them with a feeling of dread, but I knew they would help build our business and our brand. I also thought that, as uncomfortable as I was with doing them, they were opportunities for me to grow both personally and profession- ally. Like anything else in life, I figured that public speaking was just a skill that required practice on a regular basis. Each speech I gave was just another practice session.

During my first year of public speaking, I was diligent about writing out my speeches beforehand and memorizing them. It took a lot of time to do, and I would never sleep well the night before my talks. Sometimes, while giving the speech, I would accidentally skip over or forget a sentence or an entire paragraph, which would leave me temporarily flustered on stage as I racked my brain trying to remember the lines I had practiced the night before.

With each speech, I found myself slowly improving. But I still didn't enjoy the actual speaking itself. Even though my speaking was helping build the Zappos brand, I thought that maybe I just wasn't meant to be a public speaker because I was so uncomfortable with the process, even after having done it for a year.

And then one day, I had an epiphany.

I realized that nobody knew what I had written down beforehand. Nobody would ever know if I skipped a sentence, a paragraph, or even an entire section.

I had also noticed that while people appreciated the content of my speeches, they generally commented about two things afterward. They told me they really enjoyed the personal stories, and they said that, even though many of them had already read about Zappos in the press, it made a huge difference to actually hear it come from me. They told me they could really feel my passion for company culture, customer service, and Zappos in general.

So, for my next speech, I tried a completely different approach.

I decided not to memorize or rehearse anything. I would just wing it and see what happened. I knew I had a lot of stories I could choose from on the fly to tell, and I knew that as long as I stuck to topics I was passionate and knowledgeable about—customer service and company culture—that I would have plenty of material to draw from to fill the time.

When I finally got on stage, I still had some jitters for the first minute or two as I adjusted to the audience and the room. After that, the time just flew by. The audience was more engaged than they had been in my previous talks. I even managed to get some unexpected laughs from moments in my stories when I was just trying to tell a story instead of trying to recite lines from a script I'd written.

I would later learn that I had achieved the state of *flow*. In his book by the same name, researcher Mihaly Csikszentmihalyi describes flow as a type of happiness, in which someone loses sense of time, self-consciousness, and even self. That's exactly what happened to me.

From that point forward, I used the same formula for all of my speeches and found that most of the rest of the stuff that I used to worry about usually just fell into place. I just went by three basic rules for my talks:

1) Be passionate.
2) Tell personal stories.
3) Be real.

I made the mistake once of agreeing to speak at a conference about a topic that I wasn't actually passionate about. Even though I knew all the content inside and out, I wasn't able to speak passionately, so my performance turned out to be only okay. But it was a good learning experience.

Today, whenever I'm invited to speak somewhere, I let them know that I will only speak about certain subjects, which may or may not match the overall theme of the conference. I then leave it up to the conference organizers to decide whether they are okay with that or not. Usually they are fine with it, but occasionally not.

In those instances, no matter how much money the conference is offering to pay Zappos and no matter how good an opportunity it would be for Zappos to be exposed to that audience, I always do the same thing.

I politely decline.

Insights

As we started getting more and more speaking requests at Zappos, we started sending other people from different departments to speak as well. Just like in our culture book, different employees told their own personal stories and gave their own presentations and perspective. To this day, we don't have a standard PowerPoint presentation that everyone gives.

All the speaking we've done has led to a lot of unexpected results that we could not have possibly predicted. In addition to plenty of coverage in blogs and in the media, we've gotten to know many, many different conference organizers, which led to speaking engagements at Tony Robbins events, TEDIndia (Technology, Entertainment, Design), SXSW (South by Southwest), a conference where the Dalai Lama also spoke, and the Inc. 500 Conference. I've met many of the authors whose books we admire and carry in the Zappos Library, including Jim Collins, Seth Godin, and Chip Conley. We've had people from all levels of a lot of different companies tour our headquarters as a result of our public speaking appearances. From those, we've developed many great relationships and business opportunities that would have otherwise never happened.

We apply our core values whenever we give these talks. Rather than use our speaking opportunities to explicitly promote Zappos, we instead try to share as much as possible about how we do things in order to help the audience Pursue Growth and Learning. And in line with our core value of trying to Build Open and Honest Relationships With Communication, we're happy to share numbers and other detailed information.

All of this led to the single biggest unexpected result of our public speaking: realizing that we were actually changing other companies and other people's lives. It slowly started sinking in that we could be part of something that was much bigger than Zappos. We realized that we could change the world not just by doing things differently at Zappos, but by helping change how *other* companies did things.

It's been rewarding to hear from other people and companies about how they've changed their lives or the way they run their companies by doing things such as implementing core values, focusing more on customer service, and focusing more on company culture and employee happiness, and how doing so has actually improved their financial performance as well.

We continue to hear from people every day that Zappos inspired them to run their business differently, not necessarily because they wanted to be just like Zappos, but because they saw a real-life example that it was actually possible to run a values-based company that also focuses on everyone's happiness. They saw that it wasn't just theory, that there was a way to combine profits, passion, and purpose.

The feedback and stories we received led us to develop Zappos Insights, an online video subscription service, and Zappos Insights Live, a two-day immersion seminar. Both programs are designed to help entrepreneurs and established businesses improve their companies. Many participants are specifically interested in learning how to create stronger cultures and their own set of core values.

As we rolled out these additional services, we slowly realized that we were becoming part of a bigger movement. It was no longer just about Zappos. We were helping change the world.

Alignment

We did not invent the idea that having a vision that had a higher purpose was important. We did not invent the idea that having a strong culture and core values was important. Both of those ideas were highlighted in *Good to Great* and *Tribal Leadership*, and have been around long before those books were published.

But through tours, the culture book, public speaking, Zappos Insights, Zappos Insights Live, Twitter, and our blogs, we found ourselves in a unique position: We had scaled our business from nothing to over $1 billion in gross merchandise sales in less than ten years, we had a strong set of integrated core values, and our culture of being open and honest and pursuing growth and learning was leading us to *share*, rather than *hoard* all the corporate knowledge and learning we had accumulated over the years.

We had a tough time convincing our board of directors (who were also investors) to embrace many of our activities that we believed would ultimately help build the Zappos brand *and* make the world a better place. The directors on our board came from primarily technology and manufacturing backgrounds, not retail or branding. Some of them didn't fully understand why we were doing Zappos Insights or why we wanted to embrace Twitter (see the Appendix for the link to my blog post on "How Twitter Can Make You a Better and Happier Person"), and they weren't really convinced of the value of the Brand/Culture/Pipeline platform we were building. Many of our efforts were dismissed by some members of our board of directors as "Tony's social experiments."

For the most part, members of our board of directors wanted us to just focus on the financial performance that was being driven by our e-commerce business.

Which made perfect sense.

When Sequoia first invested in 2005, they had signed up to help build a service-focused e-commerce company. They probably expected some sort of financial exit (in the form of an acquisition or IPO) within five years, which was the time line they saw from many of their other investments. They hadn't signed up for the additional things that we now wanted to do that were longer-term strategies and not directly related to e-commerce, and they certainly didn't sign up for us to help other businesses create their own visions or stronger cultures.

But I saw the potential in what we were doing to make a much bigger impact beyond just Zappos. I'm pretty sure that my refusal to give up on that got me pretty close to being fired by the board. The five-year mark from the time of their initial investment was fast approaching. Alfred, Fred, and I didn't want to sell the company, and due to a complicated capital structure involving liquidation preferences, attempting to go public during an economically turbulent time wasn't really an option either.

In early 2009, we made *Fortune* magazine's "100 Best Companies to Work For" list. We were the highest-ranking debut in 2009. At our offices, we were thrilled because that was an internal goal we had set in the early days of the company, and it came just a month after we hit our $1 billion in gross merchandise sales goal, well ahead of schedule.

But at the board level, we were at a stalemate. The board wanted a financial exit, but internally at Zappos we didn't want to exit. We wanted to continue to build, and we were in this for the long haul. Luckily, I controlled enough voting rights so that the board couldn't force us to sell the company, but they controlled enough board seats so that in theory they could fire me and hire a new CEO who didn't care about company culture and was only concerned about maximizing profits from our e-commerce business.

I realized I was relearning another version of the same lesson from LinkExchange, when our company culture went downhill: the importance of alignment. A strong culture and committable core values are important because they create alignment among employees. I was now learning that alignment with shareholders and the board of directors was just as important.

Top 10 Questions to Ask When Looking for Investors and Board Members

1. Do you really need investors? Can you avoid funding by growing more slowly?
2. How actively involved will your investors be? How actively involved do you want your investors to be?
3. What value beyond money can your investors add (connections, advice, experience)?

4. What is the time horizon for a financial exit that your investors are expecting?
5. What, if anything, are your investors hoping to get out of their involvement beyond just financial return? How would they prioritize those things?
6. Do your investors and board of directors buy into the vision and mission of the company?
7. Would they accept less profits if it meant that the vision could be fulfilled faster?
8. How flexible are your investors and board members in their thinking?
9. Who controls the investors? Who controls the board?
10. Do the core values of your investors and board members match the core values of the company?

Alfred, Fred, and I brainstormed ways we could address the alignment issues we were having with our board of directors. We certainly didn't want to sell the company and move on to something else. To us, Zappos wasn't just a job or something to build our careers. It was a calling. We had too much of an emotional investment in the company to just give up. We had gotten through much tougher things at Zappos before. This was just another challenge we needed to figure out. So we came up with a plan.

We would buy out our board of directors.

Amazon

We figured it would cost about $200 million to buy out our board of directors, so we started looking for other potential investors. In early 2009, we started talking to various private equity firms, venture investors, wealthy family businesses, and wealthy individuals. The idea was to raise money from them for a stake in the company so that we could then buy out Sequoia and some of our other share-holders and board members.

As we were going through the process of talking with these different potential investors, Amazon contacted us. We had been in touch with them for the past several years.

Jeff Bezos, founder and CEO of Amazon, first contacted me back in 2005 and paid us a visit in Las Vegas. Even before he flew down, we let him know that we weren't looking to sell the company.

> Date: August 16, 2005
> From: Tony Hsieh
> To: Jeff Bezos
> Subject: Thursday's Amazon/Zappos meeting
> Hi Jeff—
> I'm looking forward to meeting you in person on Thursday.
> I just wanted to set proper expectations before the meeting and reiterate that we are looking to grow Zappos as an independent company at this point in time, but are always open to exploring partnership opportunities. I look forward to hearing your ideas on Thursday...

When we started talking to Amazon in early 2009, however, both sides seemed to have a different perspective compared with several years ago. On the Amazon side, they seemed to be more open to the idea of us continuing to run as an independent entity so that we could continue building the Zappos culture and business the way we wanted to. They had been following our progress over the years and saw that our approach to business was working for us. On the Zappos side, what mattered the most was continuing to do what we were doing for our employees and our customers while gaining access to Amazon's vast resources.

In our minds, we thought of a potential acquisition scenario more as a great marriage than as selling the company. Both companies cared deeply about being customer-centric. We each just had different approaches to it. We thought of Zappos as being more high-touch, and Amazon as being more high-tech.

Even though our original goal was to buy out just our board of directors and the shares that they held and represented, the more we thought about it, the more that joining forces seemed to make sense. By doing so, all parties would be 100 percent aligned, which was the whole challenge that we were trying to overcome with our current board of directors.

We had originally been resistant to the idea of exploring an acquisition scenario with Amazon, but Michael Moritz convinced us that it could end up being mutually beneficial and the best possible outcome for shareholders as well as employees. (And, as it would turn out, he was right.)

Initially, Amazon wanted to literally buy Zappos using cash because that's how they had done most of their previous acquisitions. That didn't sit well with Alfred, Fred, or myself. In our minds, that felt too much like we were selling the company. Selling our company wasn't our goal. We wanted to continue building the Zappos brand, business, and culture. And we wanted to continue to feel like owners of the company.

So we pushed hard for an all-stock transaction, meaning that Zappos shareholders would simply trade in their stock in exchange for Amazon shares. In our minds, this was much more in the spirit of the marriage that we were envisioning, analogous to when married couples get a joint bank account.

As both sides got to know each better over the next several months, our levels of mutual trust and respect for each other and for each other's businesses grew. When it finally came time to sign the paperwork, we felt incredibly lucky. Amazon was a win–win-win situation that made everyone happy: It was good for Amazon, good for our board of directors and shareholders, and good for Zappos employees. We could continue working toward our long-term vision and building our culture and our business the way we wanted to. If it weren't for Amazon, I'm not sure how we would have ended up resolving our alignment issues with the board. We might have remained at a stalemate. But as it turned out, our misalignment with the board turned out to be a blessing in disguise. It just goes to show that you never know when something you perceive as a negative will ultimately turn out to be a good thing.

The hardest part about the whole process was having to keep everything secret from our employees for the several months leading up to the signing of the paperwork. We didn't want to do it, but were legally required to by the SEC because Amazon was a public company.

Jeff Bezos flew to Vegas and came to my house to meet Alfred, Fred, and myself right before the actual signing of the legal paperwork. I barbecued burgers for him in my backyard and we all talked for a few hours. Later that night, Fred and I randomly ended up spending two hours in a recording studio talking and hanging out with Snoop Dogg. At the end of the night, Fred and I looked at each other and couldn't help but laugh. The entire day had been beyond surreal.

July 22, 2009, was the day we were planning on signing and announcing the pending acquisition to our employees and to the world. We planned on announcing after the stock market closed. The hours leading up to the public announcement were nerve racking. We had to coordinate with Amazon to get all the timing down perfectly. We had to communicate with Zappos employees, Zappos vendors, Amazon employees, Amazon vendors, the press calling Amazon, the press calling Zappos, our customers, the SEC, our board of directors, our investors, and the general public all within a two-hour window, and it had to be perfectly coordinated. It felt like we were about to launch a rocket to the moon.

Finally, at the predetermined time, I sent the following e-mail to our employees:

Date: July 22, 2009
From: Tony Hsieh
To: All Zappos Employees
Subject: Zappos and Amazon

Please set aside 20 minutes to carefully read this entire email. (My apologies for the occasional use of formal-sounding language, as parts of it are written in a particular way for legal reasons.)

Today is a big day in Zappos history.

This morning, our board approved and we signed what's known as a "definitive agreement," in which all of the existing shareholders and investors of Zappos (there are over 100) will be exchanging their Zappos stock for Amazon stock. Once the exchange is done, Amazon will become the only shareholder of Zappos stock.

Over the next few days, you will probably read headlines that say "Amazon acquires Zappos" or "Zappos sells to Amazon." While those headlines are technically correct, they don't really properly convey the spirit of the transaction. (I personally would prefer the headline "Zappos and Amazon sitting in a tree...")

We plan to continue to run Zappos the way we have always run Zappos—continuing to do what we believe is best for our brand, our culture, and our business. From a practical point of view, it will be as if we are switching out our current shareholders and board of directors for a new one, even though the technical legal structure may be different.

We think that now is the right time to join forces with Amazon because there is a huge opportunity to leverage each other's strengths and move even faster toward our long term vision. For Zappos, our vision remains the same: delivering happiness to customers, employees, and vendors. We just want to get there faster.

We are excited about doing this for 3 main reasons:

1. We think that there is a huge opportunity for us to really accelerate the growth of the Zappos brand and culture, and we believe that Amazon is the best partner to help us get there faster.
2. Amazon supports us in continuing to grow our vision as an independent entity, under the Zappos brand and with our unique culture.
3. We want to align ourselves with a shareholder and partner that thinks really long term (like we do at Zappos), as well as do what's in the best interest of our existing shareholders and investors.

I will go through each of the above points in more detail below, but first, let me get to the top 3 burning questions that I'm guessing many of you will have.

Top 3 Burning Questions

Q: Will I still have a job?

As mentioned above, we plan to continue to run Zappos as an independent entity. In legal terminology, Zappos will be a "wholly-owned subsidiary" of Amazon. Your job is just as secure as it was a month ago.

Q: Will the Zappos culture change?

Our culture at Zappos is unique and always evolving and changing, because one of our core values is to Embrace and Drive Change. What happens to our culture is up to us, which has always been true. Just like before, we are in control of our destiny and how our culture evolves.

A big part of the reason why Amazon is interested in us is because they recognize the value of our culture, our people, and our brand. Their desire is for us to continue to grow and develop our culture (and perhaps even a little bit of our culture may rub off on them).

They are not looking to have their folks come in and run Zappos unless we ask them to. That being said, they have a lot of experience and expertise in a lot of areas, so we're very excited about the opportunities to tap into their knowledge, expertise, and resources, especially on the technology side. This is about making the Zappos brand, culture, and business even stronger than it is today.

Q: Are Tony, Alfred, or Fred leaving?

No, we have no plans to leave. We believe that we are at the very beginning of what's possible for Zappos and are very excited about the future and what we can accomplish for Zappos with Amazon as our new partner. Part of the reason for doing this is so that we can get a lot more done more quickly.

There is an additional Q&A section at the end of this email, but I wanted to make sure we got the top 3 burning questions out of the way first. Now that we've covered those questions, I wanted to share in more detail our thinking behind the scenes that led us to this decision.

First, I want to apologize for the suddenness of this announcement. As you know, one of our core values is to Build Open and Honest Relationships With Communication, and if I could have it my way, I would have shared much earlier that we were in discussions with Amazon so that all employees could be involved in the decision process that we went through along the way. Unfortunately, because Amazon is a public company, there are securities laws that prevented us from talking about this to most of our employees until today.

We've been on friendly terms with Amazon for many years, as they have always been interested in Zappos and have always had a great respect for our brand.

Several months ago, they reached out to us and said they wanted to join forces with us so that we could accelerate the growth of our business, our brand, and our culture. When they said they wanted us to continue to build the Zappos brand (as opposed to folding us into Amazon), we decided it was worth exploring what a partnership would look like.

We learned that they truly wanted us to continue to build the Zappos brand and continue to build the Zappos culture in our own unique way. I think "unique" was their way of saying "fun and a little weird.":)

Over the past several months, as we got to know each other better, both sides became more and more excited about the possibilities for leveraging each other's strengths. We realized that we are both very customer-focused companies—we just focus on different ways of making our customers happy.

Amazon focuses on low prices, vast selection and convenience to make their customers happy, while Zappos does it through developing relationships, creating personal emotional connections, and delivering high-touch ("WOW") customer service.

We realized that Amazon's resources, technology, and operational experience had the potential to greatly accelerate our growth so that we could grow the Zappos brand and culture even faster. On the flip side, through the process Amazon realized that it really was the case that our culture is the platform that enables us to deliver the Zappos experience to our customers. Jeff Bezos (CEO of Amazon) made it clear that he had a great deal of respect for our culture and that Amazon would look to protect it.

We asked our board members what they thought of the opportunity. Michael Moritz, who represents Sequoia Capital (one of our investors and board members), wrote the following: "You now have the opportunity to accelerate Zappos' progress and to make the name and the brand and everything associated with it an enduring, permanent part of people's lives...You are now free to let your imagination roam—and to contemplate initiatives and undertakings that today, in our more constrained setting, we could not take on."

One of the great things about Amazon is that they

are very long term thinkers, just like we are at Zappos. Alignment in very long term thinking is hard to find in a partner or investor, and we felt very lucky and excited to learn that both Amazon and Zappos shared this same philosophy.

All this being said, this was not an easy decision. Over the past several months, we had to weigh all the pros and cons along with all the potential benefits and risks. At the end of the day, we realized that, once it was determined that this was in the best interests of our shareholders, it basically all boiled down to asking ourselves 2 questions:

1. Do we believe that this will accelerate the growth of the Zappos brand and help us fulfill our mission of delivering happiness faster?
2. Do we believe that we will continue to be in control of our own destiny so that we can continue to grow our unique culture?

After spending a lot of time with Amazon and getting to know them and understanding their intentions better, we reached the conclusion that the answers to these 2 questions are YES and YES.

The Zappos brand will continue to be separate from the Amazon brand. Although we'll have access to many of Amazon's resources, we need to continue to build our brand and our culture just as we always have. Our mission remains the same: delivering happiness to all of our stakeholders, including our employees, our customers, and our vendors. (As a side note, we plan to continue to maintain the relationships that we have with our vendors ourselves, and Amazon will continue to maintain the relationships that they have with their vendors.)

We will be holding an all-hands meeting soon to go over all of this in more detail. Please email me any questions that you may have so that we can cover as many as possible during the all-hands meeting and/or a follow-up email.

We signed what's known as the "definitive agreement" today, but we still need to go through the process of getting government approval, so we are anticipating that this transaction actually won't officially close for at least a few months. We are legally required by the SEC to be in what's known as a "quiet period," so if you get any questions related to the transaction from anyone including customers, vendors, or the media, please let them know that we are in a quiet period mandated by law and have them email tree@zappos.com, which is a special email account that Alfred and I will be monitoring.

Alfred and I would like to say thanks to the small group of folks on our finance and legal teams and from our advisors at Morgan Stanley, Fenwick & West, and PricewaterhouseCoopers who have been working really hard, around the clock, and behind the scenes over the last several months to help make all this possible.

Before getting to the Q&A section, I'd also like to thank everyone for taking the time to read this long email and for helping us get to where we are today.

It's definitely an emotional day for me. The feelings I'm experiencing are similar to what I felt in college on graduation day: excitement about the future mixed with fond memories of the past. The last 10 years were an incredible ride, and I'm excited about what we will accomplish together over the next 10 years as we continue to grow Zappos!

—Tony Hsieh
CEO—Zappos.com

Q&A

Q: Will we still continue to grow our headquarters out of Vegas?
Yes! Just like before, we plan to continue to grow our Las Vegas operations as long as we can continue to attract the right talent for each of our departments. We do not have any plans to move any departments, nor

does Amazon want us to because they recognize that our culture is what makes the Zappos brand special.

Q: What will happen to our warehouse in Kentucky?

As many of you know, we were strategic in choosing our warehouse location due to its proximity to the UPS Worldport hub in Louisville. Amazon does not have any warehouse locations that are closer to the Worldport hub. There is the possibility that they may want to store some of their inventory in our warehouse or vice-versa. Right now, both Zappos and Amazon believe that the best customer experience is to continue running our warehouse in Kentucky at its current location.

Q: Will we be reducing staff in order to gain operational efficiency?

There are no plans to do so at this time. Both Zappos and Amazon are focused on growth, which means we will need to hire more people to help us grow.

Q: Will we get a discount at Amazon?

No, because we are planning on continuing to run Zappos as a separate company with our own culture and core values. And we're not going to be giving the Zappos discount to Amazon employees either, unless they bake us cookies and deliver them in person.

Q: Will our benefits change?

No, we are not planning on making any changes (outside of the normal course of business) to our benefit packages.

Q: Do we keep our core values?

Yes, we will keep our core values, and Amazon will keep their core values.

Q: Will our training/pipeline programs or progression plans change? Will there still be more growth opportunities?

We will continue building out our pipeline and progression as planned. The whole point of this combination is to accelerate our growth, so if anything, we are actually anticipating more growth opportunities for everyone.

Q: Will we continue to do the special things we do for our customers? Are our customer service policies going to change?

Just like before, that's completely up to us to decide.

Q: Can you tell me a bit more about Jeff Bezos (Amazon CEO)? What is he like?

We'd like to show an 8-minute video of Jeff Bezos that will give you some insight into his personality and way of thinking. He shares some of what he's learned as an entrepreneur, as well as some of the mistakes he's made.

http://www.youtube.com/watch?v=-hxX_Q5CnaA

Q: I'm a business/financial reporter. Can you talk like a banker and use fancy-sounding language that we can print in a business publication?

Zappos is an online footwear category leader and Amazon believes Zappos is the right team with a unique culture, proven track record, and the experience to become a leading soft goods company; Zappos' customer service obsession reinforces Amazon's mission to be the earth's most customer-centric company; Great brand, strong vendor relationships, broad selection, large active and repeat customer base; Amazon believes Zappos is a great business—growing, profitable and positive cash flow; Accelerate combined companies' scale and growth trajectory in the shoe, apparel and accessories space; Significant synergy opportunities, including technology, marketing, and possible international expansion.

Q: What is the purchase price?

This is not a cash transaction. This is a stock exchange. Our shareholders and option holders will be issued approximately 10 million Amazon shares on a fully converted basis. The details of the deal terms and how the shares will be distributed will be filed with the SEC on Form S-4 and will be publicly available when it is filed.

Q: Can you talk like a lawyer now?

This email was sent on July 22, 2009. In connection with the proposed merger, Amazon.com will file a registration statement on Form S-4 with the Securities and Exchange Commission that will contain a consent solicitation/prospectus. Zappos' shareholders and investors are urged to carefully read the consent solicitation/prospectus when it becomes available and other relevant documents filed with the Securities and Exchange Commission regarding the proposed merger because they contain important information about Amazon.com, Zappos and the proposed merger. Shareholders and investors will be able to obtain the consent solicitation/prospectus when it becomes available at www.sec.gov or www.amazon.com/ir.

Certain statements contained in this email are not statements of historical fact and constitute forward-looking statements within the meaning of the Private Securities Litigation Reform Act of 1995. Forward-looking statements reflect current expectations, are inherently uncertain and are subject to known and unknown risks, uncertainties and other factors. Factors that could cause future results to differ materially from expected results include those set forth in Amazon.com's Current Report on Form 8-K, dated July 22, 2009.

Q: Can you please stop?

okthxbye

About twenty minutes afterward, I sent a follow-up e-mail letting our employees know that we would be having our all-hands meeting two days later. We had rented out one of the ballrooms in a conference center near our offices.

And then, a funny thing happened. We had prepped the managers of each of the departments earlier that morning to meet with their teams to answer any questions they may have about my e-mail. We had expected and planned for there to be no productivity for the rest of the day as our employees took in the news.

As predicted, employees were initially surprised by the news.

As predicted, employees had questions.

But within an hour of the announcement, our employees got right back to work, continuing whatever they had been doing earlier. Our merchandising team was busy making phone calls to our vendors and a handful of us were busy dealing with inquiries from the press. But other than that, for most people, it was back to business as usual. I was absolutely amazed.

I had been worried that employees would be too shocked by the headline of Amazon acquiring Zappos to really take in all the details that were covered in my e-mail. Instead, after the initial surprise had subsided, I overheard employees talking in the hallways about how excited and enthusiastic they were about the new possibilities that would open up once we had access to Amazon's resources.

It was an incredible thing to witness, and perhaps one of the best examples of our employees embracing and driving change.

All Hands

The room was packed. I was on stage at our all-hands meeting, looking over a crowd of seven hundred Zappos employees. Alfred and Fred were on stage with me, along with a couple of people from Amazon.

Party music filled the room as employees streamed in looking for empty seats. I could feel the buzz and excitement in the air. Some employees brought beach balls and started throwing them around into the crowd. It felt like we were at a rock concert and a rave, combined.

We announced that we were going to start the meeting, and everyone cheered and started clapping. The energy in the room was amazing.

We spent about an hour covering everything that was in the e-mail I had sent out two days earlier and answered additional questions our employees had. Amazon also answered some of the questions to give their perspective on everything.

"I get asked by a lot by people what we would do differently if we had to do Zappos all over again," I said to the crowd. "There's actually not much that I wish we would have done differently. We've made a lot of mistakes along the way, but learning from those mistakes has made us that much stronger. But I do wish that we could have done things faster."

And then I summed everything up in one sentence: "Getting married to Amazon will allow us to fulfill our vision of delivering happiness to the world that much faster."

As a surprise to our employees, Alfred and I announced that we were personally paying for and giving every employee a Kindle, Amazon's electronic book reader. And then, as a final surprise, we also announced that Amazon was paying for a big bonus to all of our existing employees to thank everyone for their hard work.

Without any prompting, everyone in the entire room spontaneously jumped from their seats, standing up cheering and clapping. A lot of them even had tears of happiness streaming down their faces. Just like we surprise many of our loyal repeat customers with unexpected upgrades to overnight shipping, we had just made our already happy employees even happier with the surprise bonus.

To me, that one moment represented success far beyond what I could have possibly imagined would be achievable ten years ago.

It wasn't just about the Kindle or the bonus. Those were just... bonuses.

The moment signified far more than that. The unified energy and emotion of everyone in the room was not just about my own personal happiness, and not just about the happiness of Zappos employees. We were about much more than just profits and passion. Collectively, this marked the beginning of the next leg of our journey to help change the world.

Half intentionally and half by luck, we had found our path to profits, passion, and purpose.

We had found our path to delivering happiness.

Halloween Toast

On October 31, at 11:59 PM Pacific Time, after months of waiting for regulatory approval, the deal with Amazon officially closed. The total value of the transaction for Zappos shareholders was over $1.2 billion, based on Amazon's closing stock price the day before.

I happened to be in New Delhi, India, at the time. Alfred, Fred, and I had scheduled a conference call together to commemorate the event. In Zappos tradition, we had planned to take a shot of Grey Goose vodka together over the phone.

"What should we toast to?" Alfred asked.

For some reason, the first thing that came to my mind was Buzz Lightyear from the movie *Toy Story*.

"To infinity and beyond!" I said.

We all toasted. It was official. Zappos and Amazon were married. We could finally start working together to combine our respective strengths of art and science, of high-touch and high-tech.

We were excited about the possibilities of what was yet to come.

We were excited about what we were about to build together.

The future was waiting for us.

*No matter what your past has been, you have
a spotless future.*
—AUTHOR UNKNOWN

In 2010, Zappos moved up 8 slots and was ranked number 15 in *Fortune* magazine's annual "Best Companies to Work For" list.

In 2011, Zappos moved up another 9 slots to number 6 on the list.

Zappos continues to be run independently, with its own unique brand, culture, and way of doing business.

7

End Game

Delivering Happiness

So far, this book has been about me, about Zappos, and about some of the lessons we've learned along the way.

So far, you've been a passive reader.

As we near the final pages of this book, I'd like to ask you to actively participate and think about the answer to this question:

"What is your goal in life?"

When I ask different people this question, I get a lot of different answers. Some people say they want to start a company. Other people say they want to find a boyfriend or girlfriend. Others say they want to get healthy.

Whatever your response is, I'd like you to think about your answer to the follow-up question:

"Why?"

Depending on what they said before, people might say they want to retire early, or find a soulmate, or run faster.

Again, whatever your response to the previous question was, I'd like you to ask yourself:

"Why?"

The next set of answers people give might be so they can

spend more time with their family, or get married, or run a marathon.

What's interesting is that if you keep asking yourself "Why?" enough times, you'll find yourself arriving at the same answer that most people do when they repeatedly ask themselves why they are doing what they are doing: They believe that whatever they are pursuing in life will ultimately make them happier.

In the end, it turns out that we're all taking different paths in pursuit of the same goal: happiness.

WHAT IS YOUR GOAL IN LIFE?

GROW A COMPANY	GET A GREAT JOB	FIND A GIRLFRIEND/ BOYFRIEND	BE HEALTHY
WHY?	WHY?	WHY?	WHY?
RETIRE EARLY	MAKE MONEY	FIND A SOULMATE	RUN FASTER
WHY?	WHY?	WHY?	WHY?
SPEND TIME WITH FAMILY	BUY A HOME	GET MARRIED	RUN A MARATHON

WHY?

HAPPINESS

In 2007, I started getting interested in learning more about the science of happiness. I learned that it was a relatively new research field known as positive psychology. Prior to 1998, almost all psychology was about trying to figure out how to get people who had something wrong with them more normal. But most psychologists and researchers never bothered to examine what would make normal people happier.

I started reading more and more books and articles about the science of happiness including *Happiness Hypothesis* and *Happier*. Initially, it was just a side hobby and interest of mine that had nothing to do with Zappos.

And then one day, it hit me. It had everything to do with Zappos. (In retrospect, it seems so obvious, but it took me over a year to figure this out.)

We've always had customers tell us that they think of the experience of opening up a Zappos shipment as "Happiness in a Box." Whether it's the happiness that customers feel when they receive the perfect pair of shoes or the perfect outfit, or the happiness that customers feel from our surprise upgrades to overnight shipping or when they talk to someone on our Customer Loyalty Team, or the happiness that employees feel from being part of a culture whose values match their own personal values—the thing that ties all of these things together is happiness.

In 2009, we expanded our vision and purpose to a simple statement:

Zappos is about delivering happiness to the world.

It's been interesting to look at the evolution of the Zappos brand promise over the years:

1999—Largest Selection of Shoes
2003—Customer Service
2005—Culture and Core Values as Our Platform
2007—Personal Emotional Connection
2009—Delivering Happiness

From my perspective, it seemed to make sense to try to learn more about the science of happiness so that the knowledge could be applied to running our business. We could learn about some of the science behind how to make customers and employees happier. Today, we even offer a Science of Happiness class to our employees.

As I studied the field more, I learned that one of the consistent findings from the research was that people are very bad at predicting what will actually bring them sustained happiness. Most people go through their lives thinking, *When I get ___, I will be happy,* or *When I achieve ___, I will be happy.*

In fact, the research shows that the happiness they thought they would achieve fades fairly quickly. For example, there have been studies on lottery winners that compare their happiness levels right before winning the lottery with their happiness levels a year later. The studies generally find that a person's happiness level reverts back to wherever it was before.

To me, learning about this phenomenon was incredibly interesting. It meant that for most people, finally achieving their goal in life, whatever it was—whether it was making money, getting married, or running faster—would not actually bring them sustained happiness. And yet, many people have spent their entire lives pursuing what they thought would make them happy.

The question for you to ask yourself is whether what you think you want to pursue will actually get you the happiness you think it will get you.

If the ultimate goal is happiness, then wouldn't it make sense for you to study and learn more about the science of happiness so that you can apply the research that's already been done to your own life?

With just a little bit of knowledge based on the findings from scientific research, how much happier could you be?

How much happier could your customers and employees be if you applied the knowledge to your company? How much healthier would your business be as a result?

I ran my first marathon in 2006. Prior to that, I had never run more than a mile in my life. Like summiting Kilimanjaro, it was something that I just wanted to check off my list of things to do. I didn't know anything about how to train for a marathon, so I started reading articles and books about it.

As it turned out, there had been plenty of research done about the science of running and training for a marathon. I had initially assumed that I would have to run really hard for several months every day in order to achieve the best results in the marathon, but that turned out not to be the case.

In fact, the research has shown that the best way to train for a marathon is to do long runs at a *slower* pace than you would actually run the marathon at. A rule of thumb is to run slow enough so that you can comfortably carry on a long conversation without being out of breath. When I tried to do that the first time, it felt almost uncomfortably slow. This training strategy is now accepted as common knowledge among marathon runners, but for the rest of us it can seem pretty counterintuitive.

Just like we instinctually know how to run, we instinctually think we know what will make us happy. But research has shown that you can perform better in a marathon if you train yourself in ways that may initially seem to go against your gut instinct. Similarly, research in the science of happiness has shown that there are things that can make you happier that you may not realize will actually make you happier. And the reverse is true as well: There are things that you think will make you happy but actually won't in the long run.

I don't claim to be an expert in the field of the science of happiness. I've just been reading books and articles about it because I find the topic really interesting. So I wanted to briefly share some of the frameworks of happiness that I personally found the most useful in helping shape my thinking, with the goal of whetting your appetite to do a little bit of reading yourself so that you can maximize your own personal level of happiness.

Happiness Framework 1

Happiness is really just about four things: perceived control, perceived progress, connectedness (number and depth of your relationships), and vision/meaning (being part of something bigger than yourself).

HAPPINESS FRAMEWORK 1

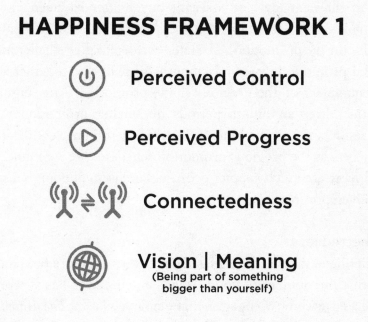

What's interesting about this framework is that you can apply these concepts to your business as well.

Perceived Control

In our call center, we used to give raises once a year to our reps, which they didn't really have any control over. We later decided to implement a "skill sets" system instead. We have about twenty different skill sets (analogous to merit badges in the Boy Scouts), with a small bump in pay associated with each of the skill sets. It's up to each individual rep to decide whether to get trained and certified on each of the skill sets. If someone chooses not to get any, then he or she simply stays at the same pay level. If someone is ambitious and wants to gain all twenty skill sets, then we let the rep decide on the right pace to achieve that. We've since found that our call center reps are much happier being in control of their pay and which skill sets to attain.

Perceived Progress

In our merchandising department at Zappos, we used to promote employees from the entry-level position of merchandising assistant to the next level of assistant buyer after eighteen months of employment (assuming that they met all the requirements to qualify for the promotion). We later decided to give smaller incremental promotions every six months instead that together were the equivalent of the previous single promotion. After eighteen months (three six-month periods of smaller promotions), the end result was still the same—in terms of training, certification, and pay—as the previous promotion schedule. We've found that employees are much happier because there is an ongoing sense of perceived progress.

Connectedness

Studies have shown that engaged employees are more productive, and that the number of good friends an employee has at work is correlated with how engaged that employee is. In *The Happiness Hypothesis*, author Jonathan Haidt concludes that happiness doesn't come primarily from within but, rather, *from between*. This is one of the reasons why we place so much emphasis on company culture at Zappos.

Vision/Meaning

Both *Good to Great* and *Tribal Leadership* discuss how a company with a vision that has a higher purpose beyond just money, profits, or being number one in a market is an important element of what separates a great company (in terms of long-term financial performance) from a good one.

Happiness Framework 2

Chip Conley's book *Peak* does an excellent job of describing how Maslow's Hierarchy can be condensed to three levels for business purposes and applied to customers, employees, and investors. The fundamental premise behind Maslow's Hierarchy of human needs is that once a person's survival needs are met (food, safety, shelter, water, etc.), then humans are more motivated by other non-materialistic needs such as social status, achievement, and creativity.

> Customers: Meets expectations → Meets desires → Meets unrecognized needs
> Employees: Money → Recognition → Meaning
> Investors: Transaction Alignment → Relationship Alignment → Legacy

Many companies and managers believe that giving employees more money will make them happier, whereas most HR surveys show that once people's basic needs are met, money is farther down the list of importance than intangibles such as the quality of the relationship with one's manager and professional growth opportunities.

At Zappos, an example of the customer hierarchy at work would be:

- Receives correct item (meets expectations).
- Free shipping (meets desires).
- Surprise upgrade to overnight shipping (meets unrecognized needs).

MASLOW'S HIERARCHY

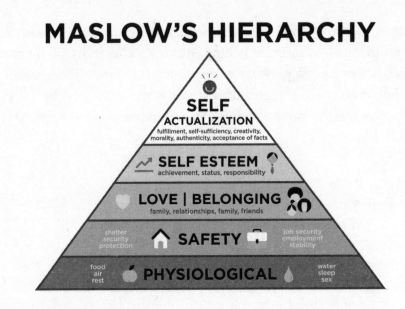

Happiness Framework 3: Three Types of Happiness:
Pleasure, Passion, and Higher Purpose[*]

Pleasure

The pleasure type of happiness is about always chasing the next high. I like to refer to it as the "Rock Star" type of happiness because it's great if you can have a constant inflow of stimuli, but it's very hard to maintain unless you're living the lifestyle of a rock star. Research has shown that of the three types of happiness, this is the shortest lasting. As soon as the source of stimuli goes away, people's happiness levels drop immediately.

Passion

The passion type of happiness is also known as flow, where peak performance meets peak engagement, and time flies by. Research has shown that of the three types of happiness, this is the second

---

[*]These three types of happiness are described in *Authentic Happiness,* but the labels have been changed based on how we talk about them at Zappos.

longest lasting. Professional athletes sometimes refer to this state as "being in the zone."

Higher Purpose

The higher-purpose type of happiness is about being part of something bigger than yourself that has meaning to you. Research has shown that of the three types of happiness, this is the longest lasting.

3 TYPES OF HAPPINESS

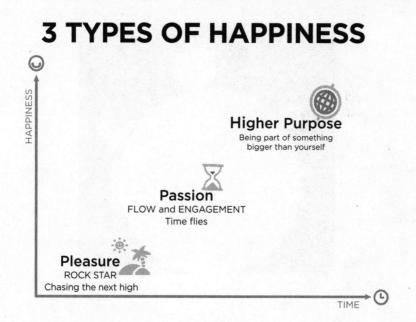

What I find interesting is that many people go through life chasing after the pleasure type of happiness, thinking that once they are able to sustain that, then they will worry about the passion and, if they get around to it, look for their higher purpose.

Based on the findings of the research, however, the proper strategy would be to figure out and pursue the higher purpose first (since it is the longest-lasting type of happiness), then layer on top of that the passion, and then add on top of that the pleasure type of happiness.

Happiness as a Fractal

According to Merriam-Webster, a fractal is "any irregular curves or shapes for which any chosen part is similar in shape to a given larger or smaller part when magnified or reduced to the same size."

Here is one example of a fractal (*Winter Wonderland*, by Dr. Ken Schwartz):

One of the properties of fractals is that if you zoom in or zoom out, the picture looks the same or very similar. According to Wikipedia, many natural objects have fractal-like properties, including clouds, mountain ranges, lightning bolts, coastlines, snowflakes, various vegetables (cauliflower and broccoli), and animal coloration patterns.

I think the parallels between what the research has found makes people happy (pleasure, passion, purpose) and what the research has found makes for great long-term companies (profits, passion, purpose) makes for one of the most interesting fractals I've ever come across.

THE PARALLELS OF A GREAT
BUSINESS AND HAPPINESS

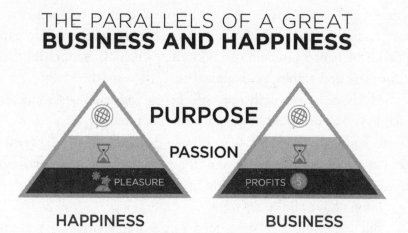

At first glance, the patterns generated by geometric fractals may appear infinitely complex, but it's often just a simple mathematical formula that generates them.

Similarly, setting out to create a great long-term company may seem to be an overwhelmingly daunting task at first, but using happiness as an organizing principle can help guide you along the way.

Even though writing a book was one of the things that I wanted to check off of my list of things to do, this book wasn't written just for that reason.

And even though this book will serve as a handbook for future Zappos employees (and maybe get us a few additional customers as well), this book wasn't written for the benefit of Zappos either.

I wanted to write this book for a different reason: to contribute to a happiness movement to help make the world a better place.

My hope is that through this book, established businesses will look to change the way they are doing things, and entrepreneurs will be inspired to start new companies with happiness at the core of their business models, taking with them some of the lessons I've learned personally as well as the lessons that we've collectively learned at Zappos. My hope is that more and more companies will start to apply some of the findings coming out of the research in the science of happiness field to make their business better and their customers and employees happier.

My hope is this will not only bring *you* happiness, but also enable you to bring other people more happiness.

If happiness is everyone's ultimate goal, wouldn't it be great if we could change the world and get everyone and every business thinking in that context and that framework?

I don't have all the answers.

But hopefully I've succeeded in getting you to start asking yourself the right questions.

> Are you working toward maximizing your happiness each day?
> What is the net effect of your existence on the total amount of happiness in the world each day?
> What are your values?
> What are you passionate about?
> What inspires you?
> What is your goal in life?
> What are your company's values?
> What is your company's higher purpose?
> What is *your* higher purpose?

> *When you walk with purpose, you collide with destiny.*
> —BERTICE BERRY

I hope reading this book has inspired you to...

...make your customers happier (through better customer service), or...

...make your employees happier (by focusing more on company culture), or...

...make yourself happier (by learning more about the science of happiness).

If this book has inspired any of the above, then I'll have done my part in helping both Zappos and myself achieve *our* higher purpose: *delivering happiness to the world*.

Epilogue

Join the Movement

As a guiding principle in life for anything I do, I try to ask myself, *What would happen if everyone in the world acted in the same way? What would the world look like? What would the net effect be on the overall happiness in the world?*

This thought experiment has been useful to me when thinking about whether to share how we do things at Zappos, or whether to get upset at the waitress who accidentally got my order wrong, or whether to hold the door open for a stranger who's a slightly inconvenient distance away.

The same questions are just as important for deciding what *not* to do, even if not doing anything is the default choice.

The ideas from this book could end here. You can choose to close the book and do nothing and move on with the rest of your life.

Or you can be a part of a movement to help make the world a happier and better place. The choice is yours.

Visit us online at:

www.deliveringhappiness.com/jointhemovement

Learn what else you can do to be a part of the movement.

Together, we can change the world.

Thousands of candles can be lit from a single candle,
and the life of the candle will not be shortened. Happiness
never decreases by being shared.
—BUDDHA

Tweets to Live By

- "Life isn't about finding yourself. Life is about creating yourself."

  —George Bernard Shaw

- "It is amazing what you can accomplish if you do not care who gets the credit."

  —H. S. Truman

- "We either make ourselves miserable or we make ourselves strong. The amount of work is the same."

  —Carlos Castaneda

- "What lies behind us and what lies before us are tiny matters compared to what lies within us."

  —Ralph Waldo Emerson

Appendix: Online Resources

- Web site for this book:
  http://www.deliveringhappiness.com

- Additional stories for which we didn't have room in the book:
  http://www.deliveringhappiness.com/stories

- Book recommendations:
  http://www.deliveringhappiness.com/books

- Zappos core values:
  http://www.deliveringhappiness.com/zappos-core-values

- How to create committable core values for your organization:
  http://www.deliveringhappiness.com/core-values

- "How Twitter Can Make You a Better and Happier Person":
  http://www.deliveringhappiness.com/twitter-better

- Follow me on Twitter (@zappos):
  http://twitter.com/zappos

- Public mentions of Zappos and our employees' tweets:
  http://twitter.zappos.com

- Photos and videos of Zappos culture:
  http://blogs.zappos.com

- More information about Zappos:
  http://about.zappos.com

- Zappos Insights video subscription service for entrepreneurs and businesses:
  http://www.zapposinsights.com

- Zappos job opportunities:
  http://jobs.zappos.com

- Culture book (please include physical mailing address):
  ceo@zappos.com

- Tours of Zappos headquarters in Las Vegas:
  http://tours.zappos.com

Index

alignment
    Amazon's acquisition of Zappos and, 213,
        216, 219
    board of directors and, 209, 210–11, 213, 214
    core values and, 208–9, 210
    happiness of investors and, 235
Amazon
    customer service and, 128, 213, 218, 222
    dot-com boom and, 44
    long-term thinking and, 219
Amazon's acquisition of Zappos
    alignment and, 213, 216, 219
    announcement of, 1–2, 203, 214
    branding of Zappos and, 215, 216–18,
        219, 221
    company culture of Zappos and, 213, 214,
        215, 216–17, 218, 219, 221, 222
    customer service at Zappos and, 214, 218,
        219, 221, 222
    employees and, 213, 214, 215–26, 227
    independence of Zappos and, 212–13, 216, 219
    SEC and, 214, 217, 220, 223, 226
AMC in San Francisco, lofts above, 55–56,
    76–77, 83, 85–86
Asian American culture, 7–10, 23
Ask Anything (employee newsletter), 136
Authentic Happiness (Seligman), 236n

B2C (business-to-consumer) companies, 94
"Bald & Blue" day, 148, 149
Bartiromo, Maria, 163
BASIC computer programming, 15
BBN, 26–27
BBSs (Bulletin Board Systems), 15–18

BCP (Brand, Culture, and Pipeline), 137, 138,
    141, 196–200, 209
Ben-Shahar, Tal, *Happier*, 230
Berry, Bertice, 240
Bezos, Jeff, 212, 214, 218, 222
Bigfoot, 39–40
blogs
    on company culture and branding,
        151–54, 157
    on core values, 163–68
    on layoffs, 191–96
    publicity from, 203, 207
    on Twitter, 209
    Zappos's use of, 208
board members, questions to ask when looking
    for, 210–11
Boys' Life magazine, 9, 11, 12, 21–23
Brand, Culture, and Pipeline (BCP), 137, 138,
    141, 196–200, 209
branding of Zappos
    Amazon acquisition and, 215, 216–18, 219,
        221
    building, 209, 213
    company culture and, 138, 141, 151–54, 157
    core values and, 159
    customer service and, 121–22, 123, 124, 130,
        134, 137, 142–47, 152
    evolution of brand promise, 230
    poker strategy compared to, 65
    public speaking and, 205
    vendor partnerships and, 60, 61, 71, 101, 102,
        103, 104, 107, 110
brick-and-mortar retailers, 100, 101, 102,
    103–4, 192

Buddha, 244
Bulletin Board Systems (BBSs), 15–18
business strategy
  core values and, 159, 160
  happiness and, 238–40
  networking and, 81–82
  poker compared to, 64–68
business-to-consumer (B2C) companies, 94
button-making business, 12–14, 21, 22

Calacanis, Jason, 192
Canaday A Newsletter, 24
Castaneda, Carlos, 244
change, core values, 162–65, 216
Christmas in the Clouds (film), 70
classified ads, sales through, 21–22
Club BIO, 83, 86, 115
Collins, Jim
  Good to Great, 120–21, 184, 208, 234
  on priorities, 200
  public speaking and, 207
company culture
  happiness and, 240
  of LinkExchange, 47–49, 50, 88, 134
  poker strategy compared to, 66–67
company culture of Zappos
  alignment and, 210
  Amazon acquisition and, 212, 213, 214, 215,
    216–17, 218, 219, 221, 222
  branding and, 138, 141, 151–54, 157
  core values and, 137, 138, 139, 141, 154–55,
    158, 159, 165, 174–75, 177, 178, 183, 184
  creating culture book, 139–42
  customer service and, 134, 137, 195, 212
  employees and, 134–42, 149–53, 155, 178,
    212
  evolution of, 216
  public speaking and, 205
  strength of, 137, 150, 195, 203, 208
  tours of headquarters and, 147–48
  vendors and, 140, 148, 189
  Zappos Culture Book and, 134–42, 178, 208
Conley, Chip
  Peak, 234
  public speaking and, 207
connectedness, 232, 234
continual learning
  core values and, 173–75, 207
  poker strategy compared to, 66

core competencies, 119, 130
core values at Zappos
  alignment and, 208–9, 210
  Amazon acquisition and, 2, 216, 217, 221
  be adventurous, creative, and open-minded,
    168–72
  be humble, 158, 183
  be passionate and determined, 181–82
  build a positive team and family spirit,
    177–79
  build open and honest relationships with
    communication, 176–77, 207, 217
  commitment to, 157, 158, 183–84, 210
  company culture and, 137, 138, 139, 141,
    154–55, 158, 159, 165, 174–75, 177, 178,
    183, 184
  create fun and a little weirdness, 165–68, 218
  delivering WOW through service, 154, 155,
    159, 160–62
  do more with less, 164, 179–81
  embrace and drive change, 162–65, 216
  hiring decisions and, 155–56, 158, 169–72
  improvements reflecting, 160, 164, 179–80
  initial list of, 155–57
  layoffs and, 191–92
  list of ten core values, 154, 157–58, 159
  public speaking and, 207
  pursue growth and learning, 173–75, 207
  strength of, 208
creativity
  core values and, 154, 157, 159, 168–72, 181
  of employees, 96, 97
  happiness and, 53, 235, 236
  homework and, 19
  profitability and, 195
  running own company and, 10
  vendors and, 187
The Crimson, 26
crowdsourcing, 26
Csikszentmihalyi, Mihaly, 205–6
customer service
  Amazon and, 128, 213, 218, 222
  e-commerce and, 209
  LinkExchange and, 39, 40–41
customer service at Zappos
  Amazon acquisition and, 214, 218, 219, 221,
    222
  branding through, 121–22, 123, 124, 130,
    134, 137, 142–47, 152

call center and, 130–31, 143, 145–46, 147, 153, 197, 233
company culture and, 134, 137, 195, 212
core values and, 166–68, 179–80
customer experience and, 121, 127, 128, 137, 142, 144, 152, 203, 221
customer loyalty and, 139
delivering happiness and, 230, 231, 235, 240
development of, 94
as priority for entire company rather than department, 131, 147, 152, 153
public speaking and, 205
repeat customers and, 95, 98, 137, 142, 144, 222, 225
shipping upgrades and, 120, 128, 144, 230, 235
top 10 ways to instill in company, 147
vendors and, 122, 147
warehouse operations and, 104–5, 106, 107, 116, 119, 123, 124, 144
WOW experience and, 105, 144, 147, 154, 157, 159, 160–62, 189, 218
cynicism, 177

Dalai Lama, 207
database programming, 30–31
day-trading, 70
deus ex machina, 99
Dickens, Charles, 163
dot-com boom, 42, 44, 89
dot-com crash, 87, 88, 93

eBay, 44
e-commerce
customer experience and, 144
customer service and, 209
growth of, 193
lack of growth in, 164
potential growth in, 57
Edison, Thomas, 6–7
electronic newsgroups, 25
eLogistics, 100, 104, 105–9, 116, 118, 130
Emerson, Ralph Waldo, 244
employees at Zappos
alignment among, 210
Amazon acquisition and, 213, 214, 215–26, 227
business model and, 101
call center performance and, 145–46

company culture and, 134–42, 149–53, 155, 178, 212
company priorities and, 94–95, 126–28
core values and, 139, 141, 154, 157, 158–59, 160, 164–65, 183–84
creative solutions from, 96, 97
customer service and, 123, 124, 130, 145–46, 147
employee handbook, 160
feedback from, 136
happiness of, 208, 226, 230, 231, 233, 234, 235, 240
informal interaction and, 150, 165, 177–78, 179
interviews and, 152–53, 155, 170–71, 172
layoffs of, 95–96, 191–96
orientation for, 135, 154, 157, 171
pay cuts and, 96, 97
performance evaluations and, 159
Pipeline Team, 137, 196–200, 222
productivity of, 97
public speaking and, 206–8
recruiting and screening process, 169–72
relationships of, 132–34, 150, 176–79, 194
relocating to Las Vegas and, 131–33, 155, 174
rewards for, 128–29
teamwork of, 97, 177–79, 196, 198
training and development of, 137, 153, 173–75, 197–200, 203, 222
warehouse operations and, 104, 106, 107–9
Zappos Library and, 122–23, 207
entrepreneurs
business choice and, 67
"Vest In Peace" and, 50, 53
eToys, 94
experiences
creating, 86–87
material things versus, 76, 106
See also WOW experience

"The Face Game," 150
failure, Edison on, 6–7
Fenwick & West, 220
financials, poker strategy compared to, 65
flow, 205–6
Fogdog, 94
footwear industry, 57, 58, 60, 127, 193
Footwear News CEO Summit, 204

Fortune magazine, 210, 227
fractals, happiness as, 238–39
Free Stuff for Kids, 12–13, 22
friendships
    business networking and, 81–82
    in childhood, 10–11, 12
    in college, 24, 30, 31, 32, 51–52, 75–76, 77
    connectedness and, 53, 75–80
    in high school, 15–18, 75
    LinkExchange and, 39, 41, 42, 45, 47
    poker compared to business and, 66
Friends (television show), 77

Gandhi, Mohandas, 5, 7
garage sales, 10
GDI, computer programming for, 20–21
goal in life, 228–29, 240
The Gobbler, 10–11, 13
Godin, Seth, 207
Good to Great (Collins), 120–21, 184, 208, 234
gratitude, 113
greeting card sales, 11–12, 13
Guardian Angels, Boston, 27

Haidt, Jonathan, *Happiness Hypothesis*, 203, 234
Happier (Ben-Shahar), 230
happiness
    business strategy and, 238–40
    definition of, 51–52, 53
    of employees, 208, 226, 230, 231, 233, 234,
        235, 240
    flow and, 205–6
    as fractal, 238–39
    framework 1, 232–34
    framework 2, 234–36
    framework 3, 236–37
    friends and, 85
    goal in life and, 228–29, 240
    lifestyle and, 2
    research on, 80, 229, 230–31, 240–41
    Zappos mission and, 215, 219, 225, 226,
        230, 241
Happiness Hypothesis (Haidt), 203, 234
happiness movement, 239–41, 243–44
Harvard University, 23–29
Hold 'em Poker, 63
Hsieh, Andy, 7, 11, 14
Hsieh, David, 7, 14–15
humility, lessons in, 23

Inc. 500 Conference, 207
individual outcome, right decision versus, 64
integration marketing, 143
integrity, as core value, 158
Internet Marketing Solutions (IMS), 32
investors
    happiness of, 235
    questions to ask when looking for, 210–11

jokes
    at GDI, 20–21
    at LinkExchange, 45–46

Kabat-Zinn, Jon, 89
Keats, John, 20
KeyBank, 192
Kierkegaard, Søren, 90
Kindle, 225, 226
kindness, random acts of, 161–62

Lao-tzu, 200
laughter
    at GDI, 20–21
    and LinkExchange, 45–46
leadership
    core values and, 175, 177
    customer service at Zappos and, 127, 128
    hiring decisions and, 170
    Pipeline Team and, 197–98
    Zappos's leadership in online market, 127,
        128, 193, 222
lifestyle, building of, 2
LinkExchange
    banner ads and, 38–39
    Bigfoot's interest in, 39–40
    company culture of, 47–49, 50, 88, 134
    computer programming for, 41
    customer service and, 39, 40–41
    employee growth and, 42, 44–45, 47–48
    financial success of, 88
    funding for, 44, 45, 47, 49, 61, 70–71
    growth of, 47–48
    hazing new employees, 45–46
    Microsoft's acquisition of, 1–2, 49–51, 52,
        53, 55, 76
    Netscape's interest in, 49
    Yahoo!'s interest in, 42–44, 49
lofts, AMC in San Francisco, 55–56, 76–77,
        83, 85–86

Logan, David, *Tribal Leadership*, 184, 208, 234
long-term benefits, and short-term sacrifices, 158
long-term thinking
    Amazon and, 219
    short-term thinking separated from, 64
Lucas, George, 7
Lucasfilm, 20

Macleod, Hugh, 200
Madden, Steve, 189
magic trick business, 22–23
mail-order businesses
    childhood profits, 14, 21, 22
    high school profits, 21–23
marathons, 231–32
marketing
    integration marketing, 143
    poker strategy compared to, 64–65
    Zappos and, 96, 98, 99, 143–44, 157, 190
Maslow, Abraham, hierarchy of human needs,
    234–35, 236
material things, experiences versus, 76, 106
McDonald's, 27
Microsoft, acquisition of LinkExchange, 1–2,
    49–51, 52, 53, 55, 76
money, passion versus, 54
Morgan Stanley, 220
Moritz, Michael, 44, 45–46, 70, 89, 213, 218
Mount Kilimanjaro, 106, 109, 110–14, 231

Netscape, 44, 49
newsletters, 10–11, 13, 24
newspaper route, 10
9/11 terrorist attacks, 93, 106
novelty, as aphrodisiac, 87

Oracle
    daily routine, 31–32, 33, 48
    new hire training class, 30–31
    resigning from, 34–37
outsourcing, 119, 130

Packard's Law, 89
Pascal computer programming language, 15
passion
    accountability and, 186
    commitment to, 2, 93
    core values and, 181–82
    focus on, 86

investing in Zappos and, 70, 73, 125
layoffs and, 97
money versus, 54
public speaking and, 205, 206
sacrifices and, 98
success of Zappos and, 89
as type of happiness, 236–37
vendors and, 188
Venture Frogs and, 60
"Peace, Love, Unity, Respect" (PLUR), 2,
    80–81, 86
Peak (Conley), 234
PEC (personal emotional connection), 145,
    218, 230
perceived control, 232, 233
perceived progress, 232, 234
personal emotional connection (PEC), 145,
    218, 230
physical synchrony, 80
Pipeline Team, 137, 196–200
PlanetRx, 94
pleasure, as type of happiness, 236, 237
PLUR ("Peace, Love, Unity, Respect"),
    2, 80–81, 86
poker
    business strategy compared to, 64–68
    as casino game, 52, 63
    Las Vegas trips and, 68–69
    mathematics of, 62–64
    table choice and, 64–65, 67, 68, 69, 120
    venture investing compared to, 87
positive psychology, 229
PricewaterhouseCoopers, 220
profits
    in childhood, 2, 5–7, 9–14, 21, 22
    in college, 25–29
    creativity and, 195
    in high school, 20–23
    Zappos and, 93–98, 99, 104, 110, 121, 123,
        125, 128, 164, 191, 192, 195
public speaking, 204–8
purpose
    alignment with, 208–11
    happiness and, 237

Quincy House Grille, 27–29

raves, 2, 76, 77–81, 83, 86
Red Bull, 74–75, 77, 78, 118

right decision, individual outcome versus, 64
risks
    Amazon's acquisition of Zappos and, 219,
        223
    core values and, 168, 170, 171, 172, 173
    customer service at Zappos and, 142
    high school classes and, 19
    inventory and, 100, 123
    LinkExchange and, 46, 50
    pizza business and, 28, 29
    poker compared to business, 65
    vendors and, 185–86, 188, 190
    Zappos and, 60, 72–73, 115–16, 125
    Zappos Culture Book and, 138–39
Robbins, Tony, 148, 207

Schmertz, Rob, 189
Schwartz, Ken, *Winter Wonderland*, 238
Securities and Exchange Commission (SEC),
        214, 217, 220, 223, 226
Seligman, Martin E. P., *Authentic Happiness*,
        236n
September 11, 2001, terrorist attacks, 93, 106
Sequoia Capital
    LinkExchange and, 44, 45, 47, 61
    Yahoo! and, 94
    Zappos and, 70–72, 89, 93, 137, 192, 209,
        212, 218
Shaw, George Bernard, 244
shoesite.com, 56–59
short-term sacrifices, long-term benefits, 158
short-term thinking, long-term thinking
        separated from, 64
social media, 143
    See also Twitter
South by Southwest (SXSW), 207
Southwest Airlines, 68
Spears, Britney, 129
study guides, 25–26
Subway sandwich franchise, 46
success
    Amazon acquisition and, 225–26
    company culture of Zappos and, 165
    definition of, 51–52, 53
    of LinkExchange, 88
    passion and, 89
Suzuki, Shunryu, 90
Swinnurn, Nick, 56–60, 71, 95–96, 97, 98, 155, 185
SXSW (South by Southwest), 207

technical quality assurance and regression
    tests, 31
TEDIndia, 207
theater, 18–19
transparency
    company culture of Zappos and, 139, 151,
        153
    layoffs and, 196
    Twitter and, 139, 151
    vendors and, 187
    Zappos Culture Book and, 135
Tribal Leadership (Logan), 184, 208, 234
Truman, H. S., 244
Trump, Ivanka, *The Trump Card*, 81–82
truth, presentation of, 20
Twitter
    employees and, 194
    happiness and, 209
    transparency and, 139, 151
    tweets to live by, 89–90, 200, 244
    Zappos's use of, 208

UPS, relationship with Zappos, 61, 104, 144,
189, 191, 221
US Bank, 192

Vendor Appreciation Party, 188
vendors of Zappos
    Amazon acquisition and, 214, 219, 222
    brand partnerships with, 60, 61, 71, 101, 102,
        103, 104, 107, 110
    collaborative relationship with, 122, 184–90
    communication with, 186–87
    company culture and, 140, 148, 189
    core values and, 183
    drop ship relationship and, 60, 100, 101, 103,
        123–24
    extranet and, 187, 190
    mission and, 215
    payments to, 119, 124–25, 126, 128
    public speaking and, 204
    risks and, 185–86, 188, 190
    tours of headquarters and, 148, 186
    WOW experience and, 161, 188–89
    Zappos Culture Book and, 135
Venture Frogs
    investment strategy and philosophy of, 72,
        73, 87, 88, 93
    Zappos and, 56, 60–61, 62, 70, 72–74, 93

Venture Frogs Incubator, 73, 85, 87–88, 97, 107, 131

Venture Frogs Restaurant, 85, 98, 99

Virgin brand, 121

vision/meaning, happiness framework, 233, 234

Wal-Mart, 67–68

WareHouse Inventory System in KentuckY (WHISKY), 118

Web design business, 32–34, 36–38

Wells Fargo, 121, 124, 125, 126, 137, 189, 192

WHISKY (WareHouse Inventory System in KentuckY), 118

Winter Wonderland (Schwartz), 238

World Series of Poker, 62

World Shoe Association, 61, 188

World Wide Web, 29, 32

worm farm, 2, 5–7

WOW experience
communication and, 177
core values and, 154, 155, 159, 160–62
customer service at Zappos and, 105, 144, 147, 154, 157, 159, 160–62, 189, 218
media coverage and, 203–4
party planning and, 86–87
tours of Zappos headquarters and, 148, 199
vendors and, 161, 188–89
Zappos mission and, 159

Yahoo!, 42–44, 94

Yang, Jerry, 42

Zappos
Amazon's acquisition of, 1–2, 203, 212–27
board of directors, 137, 209–14, 215, 218
building relationships and, 82
business model of, 100–103, 104, 119, 124, 128
call center of, 130–31, 143, 145–46, 147, 153, 197, 233
communication within company and, 136, 140, 159
Customer Loyalty Team, 131, 153, 170, 182, 230

e-mail to friends of Zappos, 126–28
funding for, 71–73, 93, 96, 97, 195, 210–11
growth of, 136, 191, 217, 221, 222
inventory for, 60, 100, 101, 102, 103–10, 116, 123, 126, 189–90
investors in, 210–12, 214, 215, 235
Las Vegas headquarters and, 129, 130–34, 174, 220–21
layoffs and, 95–96, 97
line of credit for, 121, 123, 124, 125, 126, 127, 137, 189, 192
long-term goals for, 119–24
marketing and, 96, 98, 99, 143–44, 157, 190
media coverage of, 196, 203–6, 207, 214, 222, 224
mission of, 159
naming of, 59
online resources, 245–46
priorities of, 94–95, 117
productivity of, 97
profitability of, 93–98, 99, 104, 110, 121, 123, 125, 128, 164, 191, 192, 195
public speaking and, 204–8
risks and, 60, 72–73, 115–16, 125
sales of, 99–101, 103, 104, 105, 110, 119–20, 123, 125, 127, 128, 137, 192–93, 208, 210
Sequoia Capital and, 70–72, 89, 93, 137, 192, 209, 212, 218
teamwork and, 97, 98
tours of headquarters, 147–48, 186, 199, 207, 208
Venture Frogs and, 56, 60–61, 62, 70, 72–74, 93
Venture Frogs Incubator and, 86, 87–88, 97
warehouse operations of, 101, 104–5, 107–10, 116–20, 123, 126, 221
Web site of, 101, 102, 103, 105, 106, 107, 124
Zappos Culture Book, 134–42, 178, 208
Zappos Library, 122–23, 207
See also branding of Zappos; company culture of Zappos; core values at Zappos; customer service at Zappos; employees at Zappos; vendors of Zappos

Zappos Insights, 208, 209

Zappos Insights Live, 208